CRITICAL REFLECTIONS ON BLACK HISTORY

CRITICAL REFLECTIONS ON BLACK HISTORY

W. D. Wright

Westport, Connecticut
London

Library of Congress Cataloging-in-Publication Data

Wright, W. D. (William D.), 1936–
    Critical reflections on Black history / W. D. Wright
        p.   cm.
    Includes bibliographical references and index.
    ISBN 0–275–97443–X (alk. paper)
    1. African Americans—Historiography.   2. African Americans—History—Philosophy.   I.
Title.
    E184.65.W77   2002
    973′.0496073′0072—dc21   2001051358

British Library Cataloguing in Publication Data is available.

Library of Congress Catalog Card Number: 2001051358
ISBN: 0–275–97443–X

First published in 2002

Praeger Publishers, 88 Post Road West, Westport, CT 06881
An imprint of Greenwood Publishing Group, Inc.
www.praeger.com

Printed in the United States of America

The paper used in this book complies with the
Permanent Paper Standard issued by the National
Information Standards Organization (Z39.48–1984).

10   9   8   7   6   5   4   3   2   1

Contents

Preface

Recent years have seen the publication of numerous books and articles that have offered evaluations of the state of Black history. Those writings are a response to the expansive development of Black history and its recognition and acceptance as an important area of study in American history. Those who have provided evaluations have done so not only to offer critical commentary about scholarship and the field, but also to suggest ways in which they think that the scholarship and area of study can be embellished and improved. The evaluation, for the most part, has been favorable, and I concur. But I must also hasten to add that I do not think that Black historical writing is as critical as it could be and, in my view, should be.

This is actually a criticism that could be leveled against any historical writing in America. White American historians have always found it difficult to plunge into the great depths of American history and deal with its deep irrationalities, pathologies, and tragedies. For many years white male historians wrote American history as if only white men lived in America and made history here. They said or implied that neither white women nor Black people nor other people of dark hue made history in the country. It wasn't until the 1960s and 1970s, many decades after the establishment of professional historical writing in America, that the generality of white male historians were convinced otherwise, owing to the plethora of historical studies on the people in America that white male historians had consistently excluded or obscured.

There were a number of historians of older vintages who did not like the new historiographies, feeling that they were "unnecessarily" critical of America, that they displaced white men or belittled their achievements and standing in American history and gave too much credit to others who they regarded as not being "mainliners" or as worthy as the people dislodged or denuded. Thomas Bailey, C. Vann Woodward, Arthur Schlesinger, Jr., and others, including Louis Harlan, who had written a two-volume biography on Booker T. Washington, expressed these kinds of sentiments. Historians of the older vintages felt that "objectivity" in historical writing had been sacrificed by the new and younger historians and their writings, and what they regarded as their strong "ideological" and "subjective" writing stances. Given that the older historians wrote history that emphasized white men as America's only or most important history-makers and ignored or played down the historical roles and contributions of others in the country, the criticism has a strong risible character, and some of the younger historians have flung this criticism at them.

American historiography has been characterized by strong expressions of ideology and subjectivity since the early nineteenth century, when the lay nationalist historians wrote, glorifying white men and American history while excluding, diminishing, or vilifying others. When the history profession became fully professional between the late nineteenth and early twentieth centuries, it went through consecutive ideological and subjective junctures of writing: "conservative" history, "progressive" history, "consensus" history, "radical/social" history, and now, to some extent, "postmodern" history. All these historiographical stances were against the declared canonical position of the history profession and subculture, which emphasized "ideology-free" historiography and the principles of scholarly "detachment," "disinterest," "balance," "objectivity," and so on. What was also against the canon was that each of these historiographical approaches was a political orientation, reflecting or aligned with politics occurring at the time in American society.

Black historians, educated and trained mainly by white historians and as members of the history profession and subculture, show their absorption in this milieu, including cleaving to the paradox of adhering to the canon while at the same time diminishing it by ideological and subjective historical writing. Much of Black historical writing since the establishment of Black history as an important field in American history is characterized by a strong romanticism. This showed up initially in the 1960s and 1970s with the studies on Black chattel slavery, where the emphasis was on glorifying Black slave cultural and social development and achievements and doing less to delineate the dictatorial, oppressive, and tragic character of Black slavery. A number of Black historians regard themselves as Black nationalist historians, who write Black history as if Black people were not only Africans, but as if they, as a people, constituted a country—a "nation" as it is often put, directly or indirectly—which obscures that Black people are an ethnic group and an ethnic community in the American nation-state.

Of course, writing ideological or subjective history is not incompatible with adducing some historical knowledge and truth, but it is clear that both will be shortchanged by such limited approaches. I myself have learned a great deal about Black history from reading many of the works that have appeared since the 1960s. I have been encouraged in my own scholarship by these writings. I wish to see Black history continue to develop and be vital in America, which, in my view, will be assured by Black history becoming a more critical academic discipline. And this is not simply with respect to formal methodology, but also to the subject matter discussed and the way it is discussed. Critical scholarship is about exposing things, not hiding or obscuring things. In short, it is about pursuing and adducing historical knowledge and truths, even if they emerge in unexpected forms or land with harsh impacts.

The six chapters offered in this volume represent an effort to augment the critical capacity of Black history. There are three primary ways in which the reflections of the chapters are critical: with respect to scholarship or commentary, analysis, and use of language. These chapters are not presented to chastise other scholars, nor to imply that they have not written and said worthy things. As I have said, I have learned much Black history from the scholarship that has been produced over the last four decades, but I feel there are things very inadequately stated in Black history and that there is more to be exposed and revealed about that subject. I have always been impressed by something that Sigmund Freud once said: that ideas or intellectual positions should be presented "more or less dogmatically," to make sure that they are clear, unambiguous, and readily understood. This invests writings or other presentations with tonality. There are people who dislike this strident approach, preferring a softer more nuanced articulation. But the truth is that critical scholarship or exposition of any kind is tonal, and inescapably so. If what one says as a historian (in my case, a historical sociologist) is predicated on evidence, is truthful (to the best of one's understanding), and is of a necessary character, then maybe the tone of the scholarship will seem less shrill to readers. This is the hope I hold out for this collection.

Chapter 1

What Is Black History?

This question may seem irrelevant, even ridiculous, because it seems such an obvious reference to Black history in the United States. But the question is not so spurious and the answer is not so obvious. As seen, I spelled Black history with a capital *B*. I could have spelled it with a small *b*, as black history. A capital *B* and a small *b* denote two different kinds of spellings with two different meanings. Capitalized *B* is nominative, while a small *b* is adjectival. The capitalized word Black is a reference to ethnicity, a Black ethnic identity and the Black ethnic group. The lower-case spelling, black, is a descriptive adjective, in the case of Black people a reference to their color or other biological or racial features, and thus to the black race. A race is made up of ethnic groups, groups within the same race that are historical, have a separate identity, culture, and social life, and often have a separate language. Although of the same race, ethnic groups can vary in their racial features, which indicates that race is not a pure reality. The only pure race that has ever existed was the original human race, which originated in Africa hundreds of thousands of years ago. This race was the black race, which existed in Africa for scores of millennia before migrating to other parts of the world and differentiating into different races.

Black ethnic history in the United States would not be the same as black racial history or the history of the black race in the country. There are Black people in this country and there are black people. The former is part of the latter, but the latter does not constitute the former. Black people in America, the Black ethnic group, are descendants of the black African slaves that were brought to North America between the seventeenth and nineteenth centuries and their progeny and immediate Black descendants, indicating that an ethnic group had been forged from the original black ancestors. A multitude of black ethnic groups were brought from Africa to the Western Hemisphere. They were made slaves of colonies, and after slavery ended, became black citizens of different countries, some of them predominantly black countries (namely, in the West Indies), and assumed national names and identities. When these black people came to the United States and became American citizens, their national identities were converted into ethnic identities, such as Jamaican, Barbadian, or Trinidadian. When black people came from Africa to the United States, such as Nigerians, Ghanians, and Liberians, and became American citizens, and those national identities were converted to ethnic identities.

There are numerous black ethnic groups in America, but there is only one Black ethnic group. This matter would be permanently clarified if the other black people in the country referred to themselves, in most instances, as Jamaicans, Barbadians, or Nigerians. But that is usually not the case and all these different black people in the country are usually regarded as black people, and often as Black people, or Blacks, when the latter, strictly speaking, is a reference to Black people and them only. Black historians and other kinds of Black or black academics or intellectuals could have and should have clarified these realities, but they have not done so. A primary reason for this failure is that such people do not seem to realize that Black people in the United States are an ethnic group, and that there are numerous black ethnic groups in the country, even though they know there are different kinds of black people in America. It is a case of seeing but not seeing, of understanding but not understanding, of knowing the truth but not knowing it. In 1997, in *Black Intellectuals, Black Cognition, and a Black Aesthetic*, I distinguished between Black people and black people and pointed out that there were multiple black ethnic groups in the country.[1] Manning Marable made this observation in passing in one of his books.[2] But in this particular work (as in his numerous others), he still mainly lumped all domestic black people together.

On top of the difficulties already alluded to with respect to defining and writing Black history is the widespread contention among

Black and black intellectuals and a number of white intellectuals in the country that race—biological race—does not exist; that race is a "social construction," not an embodied reality. Black historian Barbara Fields[3] has exhibited this point of view, as has the Black philosopher Naomi Zack, who wrote,

There is no set of necessary, sufficient, or necessary and sufficient traits that all members of any one race have in common. There is no general chromosomal marker for Blackness or whiteness like there is for maleness or femaleness, for example. The phenotypical traits that are used to define racial membership vary tremendously over time and from place to place.[4]

Men and women around the world exhibit considerable variation (i.e., a lack of *purity*) in each case. My use of the word Black is a reference to ethnicity and ethnic culture and social life, but also to race, the black race and black racial features, or blackness, as I would spell it. The word white spelled in the lower case, in my usage, is a reference to the white race, while the capitalized White is a reference to the large White ethnic group in the country or to an even larger White Western civilizational group. Naomi Zack, as can be discerned from her comments, predicated her understanding of race on the presumption that a race had to be pure to be a race, which occurred only once in human history, although lasting as such for a lengthy period. Biologists and anthropologists who seek to be scientific about race deny that it has to be a pure reality to be so. They recognize and assert that a given race exhibits traits across the race, but that these traits also exhibit racial variation. The Black biologist Richard Goldsby (at Yale at the time) made this observation in the early 1970s: "Members of the same race have more of their hereditary components in common with each other than with members of different breeding populations. This does not mean that all members of the same race are alike. There is enormous diversity within as well as between racial groups."[5]

When race is denied as something that is real and that exists, and that people belong to a race, then it becomes impossible to write a history of a race or about aspects of a race's history. On this premise, the history of the black race could not be written, or black racial history could not be authored. And if the black race did not exist, and black racial history could not be written, then the Black ethnic history of the United States could not be written with any clarity or understanding or meaning, because the Black ethnic group exhibits racial traits. But then all other black ethnic groups in America exhibit racial traits as well: the Barbadians, the Jamaicans, the Ghanaians, and so on. This means trying to write their history as ethnic groups would be plagued with confusion, misrepresentations, and misunderstandings.

But that is not the end of the difficulties in defining or writing Black history. Another bundle of difficulties comes from referring to Black people in this country as Africans or African Americans. As said, there are Africans in this country, but they are not all black (or blackish-brown, or brownish-black, or brown). There are white Africans in the United States as well: some Egyptians, Tunisians, and Moroccans. There is a common assumption made by Black and black people in this country, including most intellectuals, that all Africans are black people. Most of them are, but there are many white people on that continent, and there is extensive racial mixture there. Arabs are the dominant population of northern Africa, and the Arabs are white, several variations of black, and of black–white, or brown–white, racial mixture.

While there are Black historians, such as Rhett Jones, and some other kinds of Black and black intellectuals in America, such as Ivan Van Sertima, who acknowledge the different races and the cross-racial mixture in Africa, this is far from common practice by most Black scholars and other kinds of black intellectuals in the country. Writings and discussions by such people usually project the absolutist view that an African is not only black racially, but is an African south of the Sahara Desert. The common understanding projected (which is a common misunderstanding) is that African culture is the culture of black Africans south of the great desert. There is the Arab/Islamic culture in Africa, and there is Islamic culture among black Africans who are not Arabs, as in Kenya or Nigeria. There are Indians in Africa, from India, and they display their culture on the continent. These various cultural displays are reflected to some extent in the United States. A number of the black African slaves brought to this country during the centuries of the black African slave trade were Muslims, as Sylviane Diouf has indicated in *Servants of Allah*.[6] The failure of Black historians and the range of black intellectuals generally, in each instance, not to recognize, acknowledge, or understand the racial and cultural variations of Africans on the continent or in America is a failure of scholarship, to say nothing about a failure of vision and observation, and also a reflection of inadequacy if not chaos with respect to Black political thinking about Africans in Africa or elsewhere.

Similar failures also exist in Africa. Black African intellectuals there usually do not extend the continental African identity to other people who live on the continent, including the Arabs. In 1963 Kenyan political scientist Ali Mazrui wrote critically of those black

African national leaders who sought to promote the concept of "African Unity," but who also consciously excluded Arabs and Arab countries from the designation. Mazrui was also critical of Kwame Nkrumah's concept of "African Personality," which applied only to black Africans south of the Sahara, and which was conceived to promote political unity among them.[7] Even if Nkrumah's concept had been "black African Personality," it would not have been as universal as it appeared, because it would have excluded black Arabs on the continent. When the multitalented Senegalese intellectual Cheikh Anta Diop talked about "African Cultural Unity," which was the subject of one of his books, his reference was to the cultural unity of black Africans south of the Sahara, which he linked to the culture of ancient Egypt and Ethiopia.[8] Today, there are black African philosophers who are endeavoring to construct what they call "African Philosophy." They invariably ignore Arabic philosophy. In a recent anthology entitled *African Philosophy*, there was only one reference out of fifty-six to Arabic philosophy.[9] Black American philosopher Lucius Outlaw, Jr. had a writing in the work that was reprinted from his book *Race and Philosophy*, regarding what he called "Africana Philosophy."[10] This concept referred to the philosophical thinking of black Africans and that of black people of black African descent in the Western Hemisphere, and was fully exclusionary of African Arabic philosophers or philosophic thought. Molefi Asante, a Black American who is a communications specialist, heads up the Africana Studies department at Temple University (which grants the Ph.D. degree), and founded the Africology methodology, regards all black people in America and throughout the Western Hemisphere to be Africans, usually not saying black Africans, but with that being his designation. He thinks of all black people in the Western Hemisphere as Africans in a different time and place. This is also true of the Black historian Maulana Karenga and the Black political scientist Jacob Carruthers, who are both members of the Association of African Historians and the Association for the Study of Classical African Civilizations. Such Black intellectuals and those who are their followers or members of the same organizations or other kinds of organizations do not recognize the concept of black African descent, only the identity and designation African. They regard Black history in the United States as African history, and also regard the history of other black people in the Western Hemisphere as African history, in another time and place.

And there are those Black historians, and a host of other Black and black intellectuals, who refer to Black people in America as African Americans and Black history as African American history. In the 1980s it seemed that a number of Black leaders and intellectuals, in formal and informal settings, decided collectively and individually to try to persuade the American public that Black people in America were Africans; African Americans, as they said. And they were going to do that by emphasizing that name in various public media. This determination and essentially silent and nonconfrontational campaign was launched at a time when Blacks were calling themselves Black people and chanting that "Black is beautiful." It continued in the 1990s when polls taken of Blacks showed that they overwhelmingly wished to be called Black and black, and also Black Americans.[11] This thinking and conception of identities is rooted deeply in Black history and life in this country. The agents for the African American identity ignored the mass of Blacks, and also Black history. Their position was based strictly on ideology, although they argued it was based on history.

The African identity and the African American identity, for Blacks in America, leads to the view that Black history is African history or African American history, and destroys the very concept of and possibility for Black history, because Black people in the United States are not Africans, but rather Black people of black African descent. This used to be a widespread understanding among Black historians, other kinds of intellectuals, and the mass of Black people in the United States. But in the 1980s and throughout the 1990s there was an effort on the part of a few Black people to override most Black people, and to use ideology to erase Black history.

What is so headstrong about all this, so acrimonious, and so hurtful to Black people is that the people insisting on calling Black people Africans or African Americans, or Black history African history or African American history, do not know that the name African itself is not the name that the millennial black people of that continent called themselves. They also did not refer to the landmass they lived on as Africa. Indeed, the twentieth-century descendants of those people did not really hear the words African and Africa, for the most part, until after World War II, and mainly from the 1950s and early 1960s on. These were not indigenous names or identities. They came from outside the massive island continent. I made this observation in my book *Black Intellectuals*, pointing out that the word African was an ancient Greek word, fully rendered *he afrike*. The word *afrike* was a compound word, with *frike* meaning "shuddering," and *a* meaning "without." Together, the word meant "without shuddering" or "without shuddering cold," which would apply to Africa. But the Greeks did not call the large continent south of them Africa. They called it Libya. Indeed, the ancient Greeks thought the world was divided into three large landmasses: Europe, Libya, and Asia. In the fifth century B.C. Herodotus wrote in

The Histories, "Libya, Asia, and Europe. . . . The three continents do, in fact, differ greatly in size. Europe is as long as the other two put together, and for breadth is not, in my opinion, even to compare to them. As for Libya, we know that it is washed on all sides by the sea except where it joins Asia."[12]

The Romans were the first to call the continent Africa, which was not realized by Yosef ben-Jochanan, who claimed that the Greeks named the continent. In a speech subsequently published in *New Dimensions in African History* (which also contained published speeches by John Henrik Clarke, another prominent believer in black people of the Western Hemisphere being black Africans), ben-Jochanan wrote that the word Africa

comes from the Greek language, "Afrik," and it was the Greek "ae" really and then you had "ida," so you had two Greek words that [were] compounded in[to] one word to become "Africa." "Afriaeka" was the Greek way of saying "the land to the south" and it was to the south of Greece, so they called it Afriaeka and then it became Africa.[13]

One can agree with ben-Jochanan about Africa being an ancient Greek word, and thus a word that comes from outside of Africa, although there would be disagreement about its construction. There would also be disagreement about the meaning of the word, because it is the word Libya that means southwesterly. But ben-Jochanan makes no reference to the Carthaginians who were critical to not of naming the continent south of Europe Africa. According to an ancient Greek and Latin dictionary, it might have been the Carthaginians who constructed the word Africa; that is, who made the compound word.[14] The reference indicates that the compounded word might have been made by the Carthaginians as a pun on the word *frike* by adding the letter *a*. In their own Phoenician language, the Carthaginians rendered the word Africa, as the Black religious scholar Robert Hood indicated, *Aourigha* (pronounced *Afarika*).[15] When the Romans conquered Carthage in the third century, the latter, according to the ancient dictionary, seemed to have told the Romans that their country was called Africa, either saying that it was *he afrike* or *Afarika*. The Romans seemed to have called it Africa, and also used that name from time to time to refer to other colonies they had on that southern landmass, which they also called Africa. It was they who popularized the names Africa and African, which other people in Europe, including Greeks, came to use, and which ultimately spread around the world. But they did not circulate in Africa in any significant way. When the Whites/Europeans conquered and colonized Africa in the nineteenth century, they seldom used the words Africa or Africans, afraid of their potential for stimulating rebellion or shouts for "black unity" or "African unity." The Arab and Middle Eastern Historian Bernard Lewis wrote,

Needless to say, the inhabitants of Asia and Africa did not share this perception, and as far as the evidence goes, they were unaware of being Asians and Africans as the inhabitants of pre-Columbian America were unaware of being Americans. They first became aware of this classification when it was brought to them—and at some times and in some places imposed on them by Europeans.[16]

When black Africans and Asians visited Europe or the Western Hemisphere, and especially the former, they might hear the names Africa and Africans, Asia or Asians, which might be the first time they had heard them. But it was pointless for black Africans to return home using the words they had learned, as they would mean nothing to the indigenous black people, and the European conquerors might well frown upon the behavior. When black people were brought to the Western Hemisphere as slaves, they seldom heard the words Africa and African, and most never did. Slaves or former slaves who wanted to return to their homeland did not know where it was, and did not know if the word Africa, when they heard it, was a reference to a country or a continent. For example, a former slave in America in the nineteenth century thanked the white abolitionist Lewis Tappan for helping him and others escape slavery, and for providing them an opportunity to return to their homeland. He also thanked, presumably, the Christian God as well: "Great God he makes us free and he will Send us to the African country."[17] A former slave in the nineteenth century who had returned to Africa wrote the following to his former mistress who had manumitted him: "People speaking about this country tell them to hush their mouths if they are speaking anything disrespectful of it. If any man be a lazy man, he will not prosper in any country, but if you work, you will live like a gentleman and Africa is the very country for the coloured man."[18] Finally, a former expatriated slave in the nineteenth century wrote to a former mistress, "I have now been living in Africa for a little more than five years; you will doubtless allow that to be sufficient time for one to form an opinion. . . . Persons coming to Africa should remember that it is a new country, and everything has to be created."[19] This former slave wrote his letter from Liberia, recognizing that the latter was a country (actually a colony at the time), but also viewed Africa as a country. The first significant Black historian in the United States, George Washington Williams, in the late nineteenth century wrote in the first volume of his *History of the Negro Race*, "Africa, the homeland of the indigenous dark races, in a geographic and ethnographic sense, is the most wonderful country in the world."[20] And Marcus Garvey sometimes referred to Africa as a country rather than as a continent.

It was in the post–World War II period, in the 1950s and early 1960s, that black people in substantial numbers in what the world called Africa and referred to the people there as Africans, following in the footsteps of the Romans who used the Latin word *Afer* for African, heard these names for the first time. They mainly heard them in the liberation slogans of the time, such as "African Freedom," "African Nationalism," "African Independence," and "African Unity." These were all slogans encouraging action to liberate a continent from White/European domination. Juxtaposed to them were nationalistic slogans related to specific countries, such as the Gold Coast (Ghana), Nigeria, Kenya, or Tanzania (the colony of Tanganyika at the time). The nationalistic slogans and banners had more meaning for the black Africans, and the national identities have more meaning for such people today than the continental identity, and much less meaning to them compared to family, village, clan, tribal, or religious identities. A continental identity is the least important and satisfying identity for any people around the globe. In Europe there is an effort to promote a continental identity across countries and national identities, the strongest effort of this kind in the world, and it is meeting with awesome difficulties. In Africa efforts to promote a continental identity in the same manner are hardly off the ground, and have not attained a strong stimulus to go any further.

But in America there are some Black individuals, including Black historians, despite historical evidence—the kind I have presented here and more—and even despite visual evidence in Africa and America and elsewhere in the Western Hemisphere, and even despite their own knowledge of such places, who insist on calling Black people Africans, or African Americans, and Black history African or African American history. It never seems to occur to them to think that if all the black people in the Western Hemisphere are Africans, then how are they to be distinguished from each other. And if they are all called African American how are they to be distinguished. The black people in this area have had similar, but also different histories. Their cultures are similar, but also different. There are also the national identities that they go by and cherish because they speak to their sense of history, pride, peoplehood, and distinctiveness. There are black people in the West Indies who could not be classified as Americans, even though they usually are by the people insisting on the classification, because they are West

Indians, black West Indians. They even think of themselves as West Indians in the United States, as West Indian Americans, or as West Indian ethnic Americans, such as Jamaican Americans or Barbadian Americans.

Then there is the great inconsistency of the people who say Black people are Africans or African Americans, because they just as often call them by other names, including, in the case of some, calling Africans African Americans. This is what Jacob Carruthers did in *Intellectual Warfare*, and he also used descriptions such as Black, Blacks, and black, and on a couple of occasions used the name Negro (pp. 133 and 137).[21] Years before that, in an influential book, *Slave Culture*, Sterling Stuckey described Black people as Africans, blacks, black, Afro-Americans, and even as Negroes (p. 250).[22] In her book, *Righteous Discontent*, Evelyn Brooks Higginbotham described Black people as black, blacks, and African Americans.[23] Darlene Clark Hine labeled them the same way in *Hine Sight*.[24] Hazel Carby centered the discussions in her book *Race Men* on the terms of black, African American, and black Americans.[25] In her book, *Shadow Boxing*, Joy James described Blacks as African, African American, black, blacks, and as people of African, not black African descent.[26] No group of people with as many names as Black people have can really know who they are. They can not really know what their history is. It is African history, black racial history, Black ethnic history, or something utterly strange, such as African ethnic history.

Stuckey said that the black people who came here as slaves came with a "profound" African consciousness.[27] That was hardly possible, since they did not think of themselves as having an African identity and did not even know, in an overwhelming manner, the names Africa and Africans. The names they usually heard were slave, neggar, nigger, negro, and, less frequently, Guinea. As seen, even in the nineteenth century there were Black and black people (Africans who had not become Blacks yet) who did not know, once learning about Africa, whether it was a continent or a country. That does not say much about an African consciousness even at that late date. Historian Joseph Holloway, who regards Black people in the United States as Africans, also and more often uses the designation African American. He also uses the terms black, blacks, and black American, as he did in his edited anthology, *Africanisms in American Culture*. He also made the following remark: "There is no land mass called Negro, Black, or Afro. These terms are hybrids, with no real reference to the African continent. The term *African-American* defines black people on the basis of identification with their historic place of origin.[28] Holloway was not aware that the word black had significance on the African continent and in areas from which slaves were taken. My Nigerian colleague Samuel Andoh has indicated to me that the word black in the language of Fanti was *tuntum*, in Asante was *tuntumi*, was *yib* among the Ewe, was *ojii* in the language of the Igbo, and was *dudu* in Yoruba. This would suggest that the black people taken as slaves from the continent would not have been offended by Whites/Europeans calling them black, which was what they knew about themselves and called themselves. Their racial blackness was heightened by coming into contact with white people. This would also suggest that the word negro or Negro, in either spelling, would not have been offensive to the black slaves, since the word meant black. It would become offensive much later in the slave trade when the word would be associated with and even become synonymous with slavery and being a slave. But even then the black slaves would be able to understand or come to understand that the words black and negro or Negro did not have to be understood as Whites understood them; that they could invest them with their own meanings, which they did.

As far as Holloway is concerned, the debate endeavoring to decide who Black people are in the United States has come to a close. He remarked in *Africanisms,*

Thus this debate has come full circle, from *African* through *brown, colored, Afro-American, Negro,* and *black,* back to *African,* the term originally used by blacks in America to define themselves. The changes in terminology reflect many changes in attitude, from strong African identification to nationalism, integration, and attempts at assimilation back to cultural identification. This struggle to reshape and define blackness in both the concrete and the abstract also reflects the renewed pride of black people in shaping a future based on the concept of one African people living in the African diaspora.[29]

I have reserved a discussion of assimilation and integration and other American societal processes to Chapter 5. There are some other remarks in Holloway's comments I wish to address now. He makes no distinction between Black people and black people in the United States, and no distinction between the myriad of black people who live in the Western Hemisphere, as if distinctions did not exist in the past or the present. In the first three lines of his remarks he did not distinguish between Blackness in terms of ethnicity and blackness in terms of race, apparently not seeing or knowing of the differences. In the same three opening lines he conveyed the impression that all Black people in the United States used all the names of identification that he referred to. This was not true. The black people who came here as slaves did not for the most part know of or employ the African identity. The identity "brown" hardly ever appears in Black slave or nonslave records. Very few Black people throughout their history in America referred to themselves as African Americans. And Holloway did not mention some other names that some Black people used over the length of Black history, such as Afri-Americans, Afraamericans, and Africo-Americans. The names Negro, Colored, and black, the latter usually in a lower-case spelling but frequently in an upper-case one, are the names and identities that are most often found in Black historical records.

The effort on Holloway's part to show a linear use of Black identity names, prompted by "changes in attitude," is also erroneous. Just as today, Blacks in the past used several names to identify themselves. In the early twentieth century there were some Black leaders, such as Booker T. Washington, W.E.B. Du Bois, Mary Church Terrell, Ida Wells-Barnett, and Kelly Miller, who tried to get White publications to capitalize the two most used Black identities by Black people, and even white people for that matter, Negro and Colored. It might be recalled that Du Bois titled his most famous work *The Souls of Black Folk*, as black was a frequently used identification in the early twentieth century.[30] But in 1903, when Du Bois published his famous book, the Afro-American Council existed. While it was around there was the National Association of Colored Women and the National Council of Colored Women. There was also the Negro Political League. In 1910 the National Association for the Advancement of Colored People was established. In 1916 Marcus Garvey established his International Negro Improvement Association and his African Redemption program in New York.

Of course, contrary to Holloway and other historians or others who have made the claim, Black or otherwise, Black people have never had a strong African identity or consciousness in this country. Other than the fact that the black slaves who came here did not come with that name and identity, most Black people who have ever lived in this country were born here. Only 350,000 to 400,000 black slaves were brought from the island continent to North America. Most Blacks were reproduced here by Black men and women. That number amounted to about 11 million people in 1910, with about 10 million Black people in the South. But North or South, Black people made history in America not Africa, and lived in American and Western culture, from which they drew cultural sustenance in a strong manner. Most Black historians, Holloway among them, do not like to talk much or at all about the American and Western impact on Black history and Black life in America, and thus the American and Western identities of Black people, which are much stronger than an African identity, which has never been strong among Blacks. If it were, then that would have been the identity that the Blacks polled on several occasions in the 1990s would have projected. They rejected an African identity and even an African American identity in overwhelming terms. For instance, in a poll conducted by the Joint Center for Political and Economic Studies in 1990, the results were as follows:

Specifically, 72 percent of young Blacks (18–29 years old) preferred Black instead of African American, as did 81 percent of Blacks ages 30–40 and 83 percent of Blacks 50 and older. Additionally, the vast majority of Black men, and women—72 and 85 percent respectively—preferred to be called Black.[31]

Four years later the University of North Carolina at Chapel Hill conducted an identity poll among southern Blacks, and it concluded that 75 percent of the respondents preferred to be called Black and viewed themselves as being members of the black race.[32] It does not seem likely that any later poll would significantly change the kind of results obtained in the polls mentioned. The phrase African American, to use Joseph Holloway's term, is a "hybrid" construction. Some supporters of this identity, including some historians, have argued that the African name is appropriate because the black slaves were "melted down" when they came to North America as slaves, and lost their specific ethnic identities, which could no longer be traced, leaving them with only an African identity. This view is fallacious on three counts. The slaves never had an African identity to uphold. The "melting down" of the various black ethnic peoples that came to North America melted them down into a new Black ethnic group. And it has to be remembered that Black people lived in a land where words were used to describe their Blackness and blackness, such as negro, neggar, colored, nigger, black, and even slave. Black people themselves used most of these names to describe themselves, reinforcing the practice, and did it over a period of centuries, with Whites helping all the way. All this, including the Black slave rejection of new slaves, and forcing them to conform to the new identity, history, culture, and life, erected a strong barrier between Black people and the original homeland and the black people there. In short, the knowledge and memories of that land, the psychological, moral, and spiritual attachments to it, while not totally severed, were greatly desiccated. In the nineteenth century, in the North especially, there would be a few Black intellectuals who would try to make their own personal connection with what they now understood fully to be Africa. But when efforts were made by Whites to get nonslave Blacks to leave America—the efforts of the American Colonization Society—most nonslaves Blacks refused to go. The Blacks who mainly went back to Africa, principally to Liberia, were those manumitted from slavery on the condition that they go there. Efforts that some individual Blacks made to persuade nonslave Blacks to leave America and return to Africa also met with overwhelming rejection. America was home, not Africa; the American identity belonged to Black people, not an African identity. Indeed, it must be remembered that in the first half of the nineteenth century white people were trying to promote the new American national identity, which had been launched in the late eighteenth century. Nonslave Black intellectuals or leaders, North and South, were determined to claim that identity for themselves and other Blacks, including Black slaves. This was when Colored and American or Negro and American came together as the full identities of Blacks in the country. This was not a time when there was an interest to claim or hold onto an African identity, except by a few people, and it is no different today.

The identity African constitutes a *retrospective* identity for black people from Africa to the Western Hemisphere, as would be true with other black people in other parts of the world who claimed or acknowledged their ancestral connection with Africa. What is meant by a retrospective African identity is black people on the African continent, or who are descendants of black Africans, taking a name for themselves that is not theirs or of their own construction and development, and accepting it for themselves as if it were their own name and identity. But in Africa, masses of black people have not accepted the name African for themselves, or as an identity that has important meaning for them. It is a continental identity, which, as said earlier, is the least important identity for people. This continues to be true for most black Africans, and many if not most of these Africans do not accept this identity seriously for themselves, preferring to emphasize their several local cherished identities. In 1991 a black African intellectual, heading for a conference, wrote the following letter to another black African intellectual:

Whatever it is, my mind keeps getting pre-occupied with one topic: "The problem of the African being." Or put less philosophically, the problem of being African.

We both know the problems and have discussed them often. So that is not really the topic this time. The real discovery is that the problem of the African is that he *cannot* and does *not* wish to be an African. Examples abound to support the above theory. So I skip that issue also. The real issue therefore is, why can he not and why does he not wish to be an African?[33]

An obvious answer to the query is that the name African is foreign and meaningless to probably most of the black people on the continent. Most do not leave the continent to see how the world's populations regard them. Black African leaders emphasize national or ethnic or other local identities. Hearing the name African or seeing it written somewhere simply would not make much of a dent, and as these remarks indicate, they have not.

Where the name African has made a tenacious dent is among some Black people in the United States, and mainly various kinds of Black or black intellectuals. They are trying to do what some black people in Africa are trying to do: persuade people to accept an identity for themselves that they do not regard as theirs and do not want in any kind of serious or meaningful manner. Black people would accept the reality of being black people of black African descent, meaning accepting the African identity in retrospect to that extent, but would prefer to be called Black people, Blacks, or Black Americans.

The word Africa is actually a problem for writing Black history. It is not a name that can be discarded, because of its worldwide usage, and because black people on the great island continent are making some effort to accept it for themselves. On the other hand, the name and identity are used by Black historians and others in America in romantic or fanciful ways, trying to convey a reality about Black people in the country that does not exist in fact or in the historical record (i.e., evidentiarily), as it is always argued or asserted. A compromise can be made to resolve the matter, and also to take some of the fetters off of writing Black history in America. The name Africa can be applied to the continent, and the name African to its peoples, black, white, and others. The black slaves who were brought here can be referred to as black Africans, and the phrases "Africanisms" or "African Retentions" can be retained. This would reflect an *Africancentric Perspective* on the origins of Black people in the United States. But then what I call a *Blackcentric Perspective* has to enter the picture. This view says that Black people are Black and black people who developed as a new people of the black race in the United States; specifically, developed as the Black ethnic group in the country. This inaugurated Black history, and made it Black ethnic history. There is no necessary conflict between the Africancentric and Blackcentric perspectives on Black history. They interact and have to interact with each other, particularly for early Black history. Indeed, black Africa continues to impact Black people in various ways beyond the early centuries, which can be seen from the Africancentric Perspective and also evaluated and utilized by the Blackcentric Perspective to safeguard the identity and the historical, cultural, and social reality of Black people.

In 1982 historian Robert Harris made an effort to establish the parameters of Black history that continues to have a significant impact on Black historians. He made this effort without being consistent in the way he described Black people, describing them as Afro-American, Black, black American, and black people, and referred to Black history as Afro-American history and as the Black experience and the black experience. He wrote the following in his article:

Afro-American historiography, with its conceptual and methodological concerns, is now poised to illuminate the Afro-American past in a manner that will broaden and deepen our knowledge of black people in this country. The writing of Afro-American history is no longer undertaken principally to revise the work of wrongheaded white historians, to discern divine providence, to show black participation in the nation's growth and development, to prove the inevitability of black equality, or to demonstrate the inexorable progress made by Afro-Americans. It is conducted as a distinct area of inquiry, within the discipline of history, with black people as its primary focus to reveal their thought over time and place.[34]

Harris took his view of Black history further. He also remarked that "Afro-American history has taken place within the context of American history, but it should not be overwhelmed by that fact." He further asserted that it was "much broader than the activities of the American nation. Events on the African continent and in the African diaspora have profoundly affected Afro-American thought and action."[35]

Harris's view of Black history appears to conform to my view of Black ethnic history, and also seems to fit in with my additional view that that history has to fit between the interaction of the Africancentric and Blackcentric perspectives. But this is only an appearance. Harris makes no distinction between Black history and black history, which would be ethnic history and racial history. He does not distinguish between Black people and other black people in the United States. His designation of Afro-American equates, in my view, with African and African American, and thus, by that name, meshes Black history with the history of all black people in the Western Hemisphere and even with black African history as if it were all the same. This was certainly how I read his remarks about Black history not being confined to the United States, and that it was "much broader than the activities of the American nation."

Black Africa and the black West Indies could have an impact on Black people and Black history, as the Haitian struggle against France did. But it could also be said that World War I and World War II had great impacts on Black people and their history here. It cannot be said that either of these wars is Black history. In the same way, it cannot be said that black African history or black West Indian history is Black history. All that can be said is that both might have impacted Black history. Whatever was taken in became part of Black history, which remained a separate ongoing reality.

In the early 1980s, when he was constructing his article, Harris was like a lot of Black historians at the time who were trying to make Black history an independent academic discipline, with its own "conceptual and methodological concerns." This was a logical development of the Black historical writing that had begun with the lay Black historians of the early nineteenth century. The professional Black historians of the first half of the twentieth century, with Ph.D. degrees, teaching Black history and publishing on the subject took matters further. The professional historians abandoned the lay historians' employment of divine providence to write Black history, but kept their theme of Black contributions to American history and life and expanded it further, producing the *contributionist* school of Black historiography. This school of historical writing was oriented to trying to help Blacks integrate equally and fully into American society, and to achieving full freedom in the country.

In the 1960s and 1970s Black and white historians tackled the subject of Black slavery, which had been essentially taboo among both groups. This kind of writing was stimulated by the Black Liberation Struggle of the 1950s and 1960s, the great exposure of White racism and Black suppression in the country, which was deemed to have had a beginning, and the growth of social history. All this helped to produce the view that Black history was about the internal cultural and social development of Black people in America. The black African liberation struggles and the establishment of independent black African countries also had their impact on the new perception of Black history and Black historical writing, as did the conferences on the African continent that brought black African intellectuals and artists and the same for people of black African descent together to talk of the aesthetic cultural unity of black people and the commonality of their history, and to speculate about the political unity of black people, from Africa to the Western Hemisphere. The concept of African disapora appeared, and more recently the concept of the "Black Atlantic," which was the subject of the black British intellectual–sociologist Paul Gilroy's book, *Black Atlantic*, although he was more concerned to show that the cultural development of black people in the Western Hemisphere was affected greatly by Western culture.[36]

This was the kind of influence, the influence of Western history and culture and even American history and culture, that Harris and other Black historians were trying to depict as being less important to Black people and Black history and the writing of Black history. They even wanted Black history writing to cease being oriented to America and its ongoing history and development, or to seriously lessen this perception and dimension of Black history, which was why contributionist history was played down. But that also meant in the 1980s that the conception of Black history that Harris and other Black historians were advocates of did not have any room for Black women and their historical activities in America, whose contributions to America or even Black history had not yet been significantly assessed. In the 1980s, until the late years of the decade, even Black women historians were ignoring Black women and their history in America. What Harris did not seem to realize was that one of his remarks kept Black contributionist history or that dimension of Black history and Black historical writing very much alive. He said that Black history, as he defined it, would "reveal" Black "thought over time and place." He could also have said, reveal Black action "over time and place." When that thought and action related directly to America, was that not to be considered part of Black history? Black thought in America was not just thought related to Black people. There have been Black thinkers who have said things about America, or American history and culture, or about issues affecting all Americans, such as Frederick Douglass, Booker T. Washington, W.E.B. Du Bois, Ida Wells-Barnett, Ralph Bunche, Jr., Martin Luther King, Jr., Thurgood Marshall, Constance Baker Motley, or Toni Morrison. Is the thought of these Black people not to be recorded as part of Black history? Are they not to be recorded as part of American history?

These two questions are answered when Black history is viewed broadly as Black American history, which makes it possible to talk about Black people and their history in America and leaves room to consider and incorporate what comes from Africa or the West Indies or anywhere else in the world that impacts Black history. The critical thing to establish is the meaning of the word Black in Black history or Black American history. It is a reference to which people in the United States? My answer is that it is a reference to Black people, the Black ethnic group; that is, to the descendants of the original black African slaves and their Black progeny. Other black people in America are not Black people, and their history is not Black history, although it has to be said that black people coming into America have always been thrown in with Black people and have even been part of their history-making in the country and contributed to it, sometimes substantially. As a philosophical, perceptual, and historiographical understanding, Black history should be understood as Black history that focuses on Black people, their identity, their culture, their social life, their psychology, and the way they have used these ethnic, group, and personal attributes to make history in America and to contribute to histories, countries, and peoples elsewhere on the globe.

Chapter 2

Race, Racism, and Slavery

There was a time when people in America, Europe, and elsewhere in the world knew and understood what a race was and accepted that races existed in the world. This they knew even if they did not employ the term race, and even if their minds and language did not give them a clear or adequate understanding of the reality. Their senses gave them an understanding, not an absolute but an essential one; namely, that there were people with different biological attributes that made them different from each other. The ancient Kemets, whom the Greeks called Egyptians, which was the name that stuck in history, knew of people of different races. Their artists drew them or sculpted them, and left this artistic understanding of this fact, as did Kemitic writing. The ancient Greeks and Romans were knowledgeable about different races, as they both recognized the somatic differences between themselves and black people, and also brown and yellowish-brown Asians. They both knew that there were variations within these different somatic or biological groups, and had names for some of the variations. The Romans and Greeks both thought the Germans were white people who differed from them in somatic ways. As Lloyd Thompson said in *Romans and Blacks*, both groups considered the Germans, indeed "the majority of the world's white people as 'savages' and benighted 'barbarians.'"[1]

Thompson wrote that the "modern" idea of racism did not apply to the ancient Greeks and Romans. Speaking specifically about the Romans and their relations to black people, he remarked,

On the basis of the concept of "race" in sociological theory it is certainly not legitimate to presume (as almost all earlier discussions have) that the issue of blacks in Roman antiquity is a question of "race relations." Engagement of the sociological concept of "race" in relation to the structures of Roman society is an obvious precondition for any confident and meaningful inclusion that Roman society was either "racist" or "non-racist" with regard to blacks or "Ethiopians" or "negroes," and even for any satisfactory explanation, for a modern reader, of Roman attitudes and behaviour towards blacks, or of black–white social relations in the Roman world.[2]

The way Thompson bracketed "race" in quotation marks indicated that he himself did not believe that race really existed. He even said, "I have never been able to understand the precise significance of that ambiguous term." He noted that if Greeks or Romans reacted negatively to the somatic or biological differences of other people, this was not necessarily a reflection of racism, and he believed, in the case of these peoples, that it was not such a reflection. With both groups he said the reaction was an expression of ethnocentrism. With his focus on Roman society, he wrote,

For instance, the various discussions have not recognized the necessity of distinguishing between, on the one hand, the kind of reactions to black somatic characteristics that are nurtured by a racist system (reactions which have nothing to do with the strangeness of blacks and unfamiliarity with their appearance in the society concerned), and, on the other hand, ethnocentric reactions to a strange and unfamiliar somatic appearance. Unlike the latter (a natural and universally evidenced human response), the former are essentially reactions to an ideologically ascribed, and so almost infallibly predictable, social significance of a given set of somatic characteristics.[3]

Saying that he was unable to fathom precisely what race meant, and also his quoted use of the word, indicated that Thompson thought of race as something that would have to be biologically pure; that is, all members of a given race having the same biological or somatic attributes. This is not what scientifically oriented biologists believe. Racist biologists who have sought to use science as a method to bolster or rationalize their racist beliefs and social behavior, and that of others, have made these absolute statements.

This showed that they were not really interested in race as subject or reality, but in their racist, as Thompson would say, "ideological" views about race, which could be rendered "race," because it was not about race. In 1915, in his little book of historical sociology, *The Negro*, Du Bois argued that races were not and should not be considered pure biological realities. "To-day we realize that there are no hard and fast racial types among men. Race is a dynamic and not a static conception, and the typical races are constantly changing and developing, amalgamating and differentiating."[4] So races varied generally from each other, and there was variation within a race. In the previous chapter, I quoted the Black biologist Richard Goldsby, who made the same observation. The zoologist L. C. Dunn wrote several years later,

Biologically, a race is a result of the process by which a process becomes adapted to its environment. The particular array of traits which come to be most frequent, and hence to characterize the group, are probably those which now or at some time past proved to be successful in a particular environment.

This then is the sense in which the word race may have a valid biological meaning. A race, in short, is a group of related inter-marrying individuals, a population, which differs from other populations in the relative commonness of certain hereditary traits.

It is true that a definition like this leaves a good deal of latitude in deciding how big or how small a race may be, that is, how many people shall be included in it, and also in deciding how many races we shall recognize. These last are matters of convenience rather than of primary importance. What is important is to recognize that races, biologically, differ in relative rather than in absolute ways.[5]

Du Bois, Goldsby, and Dunn were able to understand things about race that Thompson was unable to fathom. They said that no race was pure biologically, which also meant that it did not have stable, unchanging biological attributes. They said there was variation within a race, and that races differed from each other in relative ways. So now one has to ask what is so threatening about all of this? Why has race been so excoriated in the last decades? Why do people want to deny the existence of race? Simply put, the answer is racism and the fear of it. But this is too simple, because a more meaningful explanation is that people do not really know what racism is and how it differs from race. Thompson referred to racism being an "ideology" or belief system about fixed or stable biological characteristics. This was the same understanding of racism that historian George Frederickson presented in *The Arrogance of Race*:

"The term *racism* has become a source of considerable confusion. In its limited, precise, and original sense, racism is the doctrine that a man's behavior is determined by stable inherited characters deriving from separate racial stocks and usually considered to stand to one another in relations of superiority and inferiority."[6] But Frederickson's view of racism, which is a very common one to this day among American and other intellectuals, is not a definition of the phenomenon. Frederickson said he had been influenced by Du Bois in his understanding of racism, but he was not influenced significantly, because Du Bois always knew, even going back to the late 1890s, that what was called "race prejudice" back then was not really about race. As he said in his *Autobiography*, the white Irish were treated like the black people, and sometimes worse than they in his hometown of Great Barrington, Massachusetts. Both were treated as if they were innately inferior.[7] The Irish were the same race as the people who were treating them in this manner. Du Bois noticed how white men treated white women in America as if they were innately inferior. He even perceived lower-class white people being treated that way by the upper classes of white people. In 1912 he made the following remark before a white women's group: "Democracy alone is the method of storing the whole experience of the race for the benefit of the future, and if democracy tries to exclude women or Negroes or the poor or any class because of innate characteristics which do not interfere with intelligence then that democracy cripples itself and belies its name."[8]

When saying race in his remarks, Du Bois was speaking of the human race. But it also has to be noted that he said that Blacks, women (meaning white women, because there were women among Blacks), and lower-class white people could all be treated, as he said, as if they were "innately" "inferior." When he was a student in Germany in the 1890s, Du Bois observed how white Germans treated white Jews as if they were "innately" "inferior" people, and he saw instances of the same thing in the United States. In 1934, when he was teaching sociology at Atlanta University, he made the following remark in a letter to the Black sculptor Elizabeth Prophet: "The class has been studying race problems, more specifically the problem of Jews throughout Europe, and now the problem of the Irish. I have in all cases taken opportunity to make comparisons with the Negro problem in the United States."[9] The "Jewish Problem," the "Irish Problem," the "Negro Problem," and the "Woman Problem" were all generally the same, having their basis in the belief of people that they were all "innately" "inferior." In the early 1950s, Du Bois summed up his understanding of what at the time was called race prejudice, although the word racism was beginning to be used extensively:

It was not . . . solely a matter of color or physique and racial characteristics. . . . No, the race problem in which I was interested cut across lines of color and physique and belief and status and was a matter of cultural patterns, perverted teachings and human hatred and prejudice, which reached all sorts of people and caused endless evil to all men.[10]

What the comments about Du Bois and the quotations from him show is that he knew that what he called race prejudice, and which would today be called racism, was not the same as race, and was not even necessarily predicated on race. Indeed, race prejudice did not even have to be related to a race at all, as it was a belief system and practice that could be applied to any kind of human group, even people of the same race. Du Bois showed this understanding in another instance. In 1936 he visited Nazi Germany for six months to study the educational system there. He would later comment about his observance of the way many Germans treated Jews, who were white like they were; that is, of the same race as they:

Of course, many of the usual characteristics were missing in this outbreak of race hate in Germany. There was in reality little physical difference between German and Jew. . . . Nevertheless, the ideological basis of this attack was that of fundamental biological differences showing itself in spiritual and cultural incompatibility.[11]

What Du Bois understood about race prejudice was that it was a generalized social phenomenon that could take numerous specific forms, with racism against a race being just one form. What a racist did was to devise some beliefs about a group or groups of people that said they had "inferior" "internal" "traits" that determined their thought and social behavior. These "traits" did not exist in the people. They were fantasies concocted about these people, about the alleged "traits" in them. The concoctions were the "traits" that were "innate" or "natural," not the actual natural or innate traits, which were used as the basis to create fanciful views about "natural" "traits." This is what created the "race," something other than the actual race. This "race," with its "inferior" "innate" or "natural" "traits," was then imposed on an actual race and said to be its innate attributes that determined its thought and social behavior, and also how it made history. But a nonexistent "race" with no existing attributes could be concocted with respect to any group of people, and then, if possible, imposed upon them and declared to be their "inner" "determinant" "traits." A "race" concoction could be spread over white people, over black people, over women generally, over an ethnic group, over a social class, over any group that racists wanted to target and be able to treat in a racist manner, and that included people within their own race. A racist does not care what race a group is. What he or she wants to do is to be able to treat a group of human beings as if they were "nonhuman" or "subhuman," a "race" of "nonhumans" or "subhumans" that their racist beliefs tell them they are, while other of their racist beliefs, about themselves, say to them that they are a "race" of "gods" or "godlike" "entities." Racist beliefs are anti–human being and antihumanity, which makes racists, functioning as racists, anti–human being and antihumanity. Thinking of themselves as "gods" or "godlike," and their victims as "nonhumans" and "subhumans," removes both from the status and context of human being and humanity.

This was the broad understanding that Du Bois had of racism, but this was not the way he overwhelmingly wrote on the subject, because most of his writing about race prejudice was about the racism that white people showed toward Black or black people. But as has been seen, he clearly knew about the generalized and specific manifestations of racism. What has always been missing with respect to this phenomenon are names to describe the various forms. In 1987 I published an article entitled "The Faces of Racism" and provided some names.[12] Eleven years later, I went back to those names and others and provided a full discussion of racism in my book *Racism Matters*.[13] The specific forms of racism I alluded to were the following: *white supremacy*, which were racist beliefs about white people, and pertaining to them only, that projected their "innate" "superiority." Another was *ebonicism*, which applied to black and Black people, declaring their "innate" "inferiority." There was *maleism*, which was racist beliefs about the "innate" "superiority" of men. There was also *sexism*, which referred to the alleged "natural" "inferiority" of women. There was *anti-Jewism*, as opposed to anti-Semitism, which is not accurate, that declared Jews as "innately" "inferior." Another racist belief was *redicism*, marking the American Indian off as "naturally" "inferior." *Xanthicism* did the same for yellow or yellowish-brown people, and *bronzism* was my term to describe racist behavior toward Hispanic people in America and in other parts of the Western Hemisphere.

What thinkers in the past and to this day have yet to understand is that racist beliefs and practices are many millennia old, going back to the earliest constructions of maleism and sexism, or maleism/ sexism, as racist beliefs are devised and executed in pairs: beliefs for the alleged superior people and beliefs for the alleged inferior people. White supremacy/ebonicism have been paired in Western and American history, which has also been true of white supremacy and xanthicism. In America it has been white supremacy/redicism and white supremacy/bronzism. In Nazi Germany Aryanism and anti-Jewism were paired. The paired beliefs do not have to be articulated equally or fully. Those not articulated are always implied and always function as predicates. Racist beliefs and practices executed over an extensive time produce a racist psychology that can vary within racists but which makes them think and act like racists—the ones they have been taught to be—even when they do not explicitly or fully express racist beliefs. We are living at a time now when racist beliefs and racist behavior are both expressed more subtly. But even in times or periods of blatant racism, subtle racism is also amply expressed, as in the opening phrase of the American Constitution: "We the people."

When it is understood that maleism/sexism is the oldest form of racism, then there has to be a reevaluation of the claims made that racism did not exist in ancient times, specifically in Greece and Roman times. Lloyd Thompson said it did not, but his assertion was based on an understanding that racism was associated exclusively with race, and with respect to fixed or stable biological characteristics. As we have seen, racism is not about any actual biological traits or any actual human traits or group traits, but about *fantasies* concocted about these things that racists believe to be the real attributes, the real representations of people. This denotes the irrationality, pathology, and immorality associated with racism and the racist psychology, how much of each determined by how racist a person is. The white racist, as Ralph Ellison said in his novel *The Invisible Man*, invisibilizes his or her Black victims. James Baldwin said the same thing in his collection of essays in the 1950s entitled *Nobody Knows My Name*. What both of these writers meant was that white racists did not see actual Black people, their actual attributes and realities; that is, they saw them as Others, but only their racist concoctions of them. This also meant that white racists related to Black people on the basis of their fantasies about them that declared them to be "nonhuman" or "subhuman," or as "Non-Others." What Ellison and Baldwin did not perceive or say as clearly was that white racists invisibilized themselves as well with their white supremacist beliefs, and related to themselves on the basis of these false representations; that is, related to themselves as if they were "gods" or "godlike," or as "Non-Others."

Greek and Roman men, in a very strong manner, were maleists/ sexists. Nancy Tuana wrote about the maleism/sexism of Plato and Aristotle, which was woven into their philosophical thought. She also wrote about the maleism/sexism of other prominent white male thinkers: Descartes, Rousseau, Kant, Hume, Locke, and Hegel. Tuana did not have the concept of maleism to employ in her writing, although she did use "maleness." She only mentioned sexism a few times in her book, and did not understand it to be a form of racism. She saw herself writing about male and female gender in ancient Greece and beyond, and argued that "gender bias" affected the way the men she wrote about constructed their philosophies; that they were predicated on these biases. In the preface of her book, she said,

One of my central concerns will be to expose the ways in which such gender biases are woven into the very categories of philosophy. My point is not that we have to give up doing philosophy, but that if we are to remove the sexism inherent in the categories of philosophies, the philosophy we do will have to be significantly different.[14]

Tuana equated sexism with gender, instead of seeing it as a form of racism and as racist beliefs applied to the female gender to create a "race" that is imposed on female gender; that is, a "race" of "nonhumans" and "subhumans." Tuana used the term "maleness" and equated it with male gender. Her discussion at all times on the subject of male gender was a discussion of male gender predicated on maleism or this form of racism, which had such men thinking that they and other men belonged to a "race" of "gods" or "godlike" "entities." If Tuana had understood what racism was and had had a full understanding of it, she would have been able to see that the Enlightenment thinkers of the eighteenth century that she wrote about were not only maleists/sexists, but also white supremacists/ ebonicists, and she could have shown how this form of racism was woven into their thought.

It was in the eighteenth century and during the Enlightenment that the word and reality of race became prominent in Western thought, and this discussion of race was only ostensibly about that. It was mainly about "race." The discussion of "race" was also attached to the discussion of black or Black slavery. The Enlightenment occurred at a time when Whites/Europeans were expanding the black African slave trade and were making extensive use of black African, black, and Black slave labor in the Western Hemisphere. The eighteenth century generally marked the continued White/European expansion across the globe, now expanding into the subcontinent, or India, and also into other parts of Asia. This brought Whites/Europeans into contact with more of the planet's dark-hued people and their cultures and customs and traditions, which also led to the development of racist beliefs for old and new racist victims.

A very strong racist belief at this time was white supremacy/ebonicism. It was necessary to rationalize and justify the black African slave trade and the use of black labor in the Western Hemisphere. Both were great sources of wealth for Whites/Europeans and were indispensable to their continued modernization and development. These sources of wealth helped to augment the power and wealth of autocrats and the state, the nobility, and the middle class; the financing of commercial, industrial, technological, and scientific development, organizational and institutional development, and the development and flowering of the aesthetic culture of the area. Much of this kind of development was going on in North America, initially in English colonies and then in the emerging new United States, which drained wealth from its slave trade and slave labor to help finance it.

The science that was developing in Europe was used to help rationalize and justify the slave trade, slavery, and the abuse and exploitation of black people. It was during the eighteenth century, during the Enlightenment, during what historians and philosophers call the development of *rationalism* in Europe, beyond the seventeenth century, that races were classified. It was done initially by the German taxonomist Carolus Linnaeus. He declared that there were four races in the world: the "European man" (white), the "Asiatic man" (yellow), the "African man" (black), and the "American man" (red). He ranked these races in a hierarchical manner, with the white race at the top, the yellow followed by the red race in the middle, and the black race at the bottom. This was not a ranking based on ethnological or aesthetic principles, but rather on the basis of racist beliefs, racist beliefs that supported science and upon which the latter was predicated. Saul Dubow had the following to say about the classification of Linnaeus and the Enlightenment context in which it occurred and to which it was related:

The study of human differences is perhaps most sensibly traced back to the mid-eighteenth century, for it is with the development of the European Enlightenment that the main racial divisions of the world began to be firmly established. The emergence of natural history as a distinctive field of knowledge posed a formidable challenge to the traditional biblical account of common descent from Adam. Rationalism demanded new universal definitions of man's place in nature as well as his position in God's universe. One of the great paradoxes of the Enlightenment, therefore, is that it implied not only the advance of scientific forms of reasoning, but also "the rationalisation of old prejudices." The methodology of observation, measurement and classification were of primary importance in respect to both of these objectives.

A decisive development was the association of race as "type." Linnaeus, who is credited with having established the principles of taxonomy in the biological sciences, provided one of the most famous classificatory schemes. In *Systema Naturae* he distinguished between European Man, Asiatic Man, African Man and American Man. To each of these he attached character descriptions. For example, Europeans were ingenious, inventive and governed by law, whereas Africans were crafty, lazy, careless and governed by the arbitrary will of their masters.[15]

The masters that Linnaeus was referring to were the kings, chiefs, and others who had power over other black Africans. He could have said there were white ship captains, white masters, and other white men who exercised arbitrary and not rational power over black people. He could have mentioned that Whites/Europeans, or Whites/Westerners were governed by slave laws and racist laws. It was, of course, a racist argument to assert that Whites/Europeans were "ingenious, inventive, and governed by law" on the basis of their nature, and that black Africans or other black people "were crafty, lazy, careless and governed by . . . arbitrary will," owing to their nature. These were beliefs about white people that characterized *all* white people, and Linnaeus posited beliefs about black people that characterized the *whole* race. These were fanciful depictions of "innate" "qualities," but believed by Linnaeus to be the actual attributes of white and black people.

He was not the only European scientist or other kind of intellectual who projected fanciful beliefs about the "innate" or "natural" "qualities" of white and black people, using the words innate and natural as if they were describing real attributes and all the while believing that they were. Great names of the Enlightenment were involved. David Hume wrote, "I am apt to suspect the Negroes . . . to be naturally inferior to the White. There never was a civilized nation of any other complexion than white, nor even any individual eminent either in action or speculation, no ingenious manufacturers amongst them, no arts, or sciences."[16] Hume expressed suspicion in his first sentences, but what he felt was certain knowledge and understanding in the other ones. Thomas Jefferson made the following remarks: "I advance it, therefore, as a suspicion only that the blacks, whether originally a distinct race or made distinct by time or circumstances, are inferior to the whites in the endowments of both body and mind." Many white historians have used these remarks to argue that Jefferson was not really a racist, because he was only voicing a suspicion. He was not voicing a suspicion in the remarks they usually do not quote:

Comparing them by their faculties of memory, reason, and imagination, it appears to me that in memory they are equal to the whites: in reason much inferior, as I think one could scarcely be found capable of tracing and comprehending the investigations of Euclid; and in imagination they are dull, tasteless, and anomalous.

His imagination is wild and extravagant, escapes incessantly from every restraint of reason and taste, and in the course of its vagaries, leaves a tract of thought as incoherent and eccentric, as is the course of a meteor through the sky.[17]

It was directly after these remarks that Jefferson said, "I advance it, therefore, as a suspicion." The German philosopher Georg Hegel said, "The Negro represents natural man in all his wild and untamed nature. If you want to treat and understand him rightly, you must abstract elements of respect and morality and sensitivity—there is nothing remotely humanized in the Negro character."[18]

The French anthropologist Georges Cuvier expressed the following white supremacistic and ebonicistic racist remarks:

The Caucasian [race], to which we ourselves belong, is chiefly distinguished by the beautiful form of the head, which approximates to a perfect oval. It is also remarkable for variations in the shade and complexion, and colour of the hair. From the variety have sprung the most civilised dominion over the rest of mankind.[19]

He also said, regarding the black race,

Its characters are black complexion, woolly hair, compressed cranium, and flatish nose. In the prominence of the lower part of the race (prognathism), the thickness of the lips, it manifestly approaches to the monkey tribe. The hordes of which this variety is composed have always remained in the most complete state of barbarism.[20]

In the 1850s, as the Enlightenment continued, the French intellectual Comte Joseph-Arthur de Gobineau remarked, "History shows that all civilization derives from the white race, that none can exist without its help, and that a society is great and brilliant only so far as it preserves the blood of the noble group that created it."[21] Finally, the British physician Charles White, as William Tucker tells us, wrote the following in a publication in the early 1850s:

On the basis of anatomical and physical evidence . . . blacks were a completely separate species intermediate between whites and apes. The feet of blacks, their fingers and toes, their "gibbous" (bulging, protuberant) legs, their hair, their cheekbones and chin, the length of their arms, the size of their skull and sex organs, and even their body odor placed them much closer than Europeans to "brute creation." . . . Exceptional capabilities exhibited by Blacks only constituted further proof of their proximity to infrahuman species. For example, the superior memory some blacks displayed, White maintained, was an ability shared by a number of domestic animals, like the horse and dog.[22]

These comments not only reflect racist beliefs, they also stand as brief *racist narratives*. Such narratives could also be much longer, even book length, as many books were written between the eighteenth and twentieth centuries, the centuries of the Enlightenment, talking of the "innate" "superiority" of white people and the "innate" "inferiority" of black people, and what white people were "innately" capable of doing in the making of history and in constructing culture and civilization, and what the black race was "innately" incapable of doing. The discussion would ostensibly be about race, using that word extensively, but it was always about what underlay the discussion, "race" and its "inherent" or "natural" "traits," which greatly colored (i.e., greatly exaggerated) the discussion of the physical traits of the white and black races and what they could do or not do. It was very important to make clear to readers that black people were outside the realm of humanity, even if this were not stated explicitly about white people. This was best done, white thinkers believed, who were usually white men, by denouncing any or holding out a very limited cerebral capability for black people. For white men what distinguished humans from animals was the ability to reason. This was what Enlightenment thinkers emphasized in the eighteenth century, and it carried over strongly into other centuries.

Indeed, the Enlightenment is noted for its emphasis on reason, rationality, or what is called the philosophy of rationalism. But what is not understood about this emphasis was that it was predicated on white supremacy/ebonicism, and even maleism/sexism. The glorification of reason also carried the glorification of white men, even if there were no reference to such men, who believed they were the only ones capable of reason and rationality. They even argued, in the universal terms they always used when they knew that what they were saying was meant for white men only, that rationality was innate to human beings on the basis of their nature. But Enlightenment thinkers, as a rule, did not think that black people were human beings in any significant way, and even said so, often in the most mephitic way, so reason and rationality could not possibly be inherent in their nature. This kind of argument, of course, functioned to strengthen the rationalization of the black African slave trade and black slavery in the Western Hemisphere. Black people were not humans or full humans and they had little to no intellectual ability, so making them slaves and exploiting their labor as slaves was not as evil as might be thought. They could be made use of, and profitably, like other animals.

Enlightenment thinkers were not really interested in race, even though they classified and talked and wrote endlessly about it. What they were always most interested in, what undergirded the discussion about races and stimulated the way they ensued, was "race" and "races," or "Non-Others," things that did not exist, except as fanciful abstractions, but which were believed to be real and to be the actual characteristics or representations of the people to whom they referred. Today, postmodern thinkers would quickly call this "social construction," the social construction of "race."

Postmodern thinkers have made "social construction" an operative phrase. They arrived at it by criticizing the metaphysical philosophers, who were descendants of the Enlightenment metaphysical philosophers, and also by criticizing Hitler and the Nazis and what they did to the Jews and the way they rationalized and justified the behavior. Enlightenment metaphysical philosophers were concerned to establish, by logical reasoning and philosophical thought, *absolutes*: absolute truth, absolute justice, absolute freedom, absolute understanding, absolute reality, and other kinds of absolutes. What was established, they argued, was a priori, ahistorical, transcendental, and eternal. The metaphysical philosophers sought to produce abstract absolutes, not paying much attention to actual, empirical realities, and even often disdaining the latter. What was important to them were the abstract versions of things they reasoned out and established by what they called rational logic.

The criticism that the later postmodernists would have of this kind of philosophical thinking was that it did not relate thought to reality, nor seek significantly to do so. Truth, justice, freedom, reality, and so on were just "social constructions," "discourse," and "word games," but not the reflection of anything real or tangible. The abstractions did not correspond to the real world. The postmodernists attacked Adolf Hitler, the Nazis, and other Germans for socially constructing "race" with respect to Jews, as a rationale and justification for exterminating millions of them. From there, they argued that race was socially constructed, and extended this argument to include black people and to argue with respect to them that race—a black race—was socially constructed.

But the way postmodernists came to use the phrase socially constructed, and mainly presently use it, is to deny the very idea of reality. They had criticized the metaphysical philosophers for having ignored reality, for not seeking to relate their thought to it. They, in turn, took matters a step further, and took what postmodernists themselves have called a "linguistic turn." This turn was extreme, as it denied that embodied reality existed or that it had ever existed. All that ever existed was language: description, discourse, vocabulary, word games, and linguistic or language representations. Nothing existed beyond language. This was not only an extreme, but a nonsensical position, because one would have to argue that the "linguistic turn," or "discourse," or "language representations" produced themselves, that no human beings—who embodied reality—did so. How rational is it to deny one's own embodiment?

But the postmodernists made it appear that social construction was new in the world, and that they had discovered it. They associated it with the denial of reality, when, in fact, there is nothing incompatible with human beings engaging in social construction; that is, language construction and reality. Indeed, they are quite compatible. I made the following remark in my book *Black Intellectuals* about social construction:

Human beings socially construct everything. That is, they use language to describe, to identify, to characterize, to classify, and to authorize and legitimize. This is simply what human beings do, and precisely because they are human and precisely because human beings use language to devise thoughts and descriptions and to guide their social behavior. Something that is called a tree exists independently of that name. And the same goes for rock, brook, mountain, sky, and star. Each could have been called something else. But the naming of these things or providing descriptions of them did not bring any of them into existence. They existed before the names and descriptions were applied; this is the way of many aspects of reality. This would include race, meaning a biological reality, which existed with its characteristics long before a name and description were applied to it.[23]

Language social construction is simply what human beings do, and there is nothing illogical, irrational, or illegitimate about it. What becomes a question is how the social construction is done. Is it done to try to describe a reality as best as possible, or is it done, consciously or unconsciously, to distort or to misrepresent reality? Is it done, the way postmodern thinkers do it, to deny reality? And why is it that they want to deny race? On the one hand, they would do so because they would be making the assumption that a race had to be pure to be a race, which was the assumption made by Anthony Appiah in his book *In My Father's House*, but which is not true.[24] Another reason is that such people deny any kind of reality. But a third reason is twofold and that breaks down along white and black racial lines. So many white postmodern thinkers, and other kinds of white thinkers as well, have a fear of being called racists. The Nazi image comes immediately to their minds, and they stand in its shadow. And that is because so many have white supremacist/ebonicistic racist views that they express rather subtly. But saying that race is "socially constructed" is a way of denying that race exists. To them racism is associated with race, but if a race does not exist, then they themselves cannot be racists. It is logical thinking, but rather twisted. In regard to Black or black intellectuals it is a case of being tired of white people having the concept of race in their hands for any use, knowing how they have abused it and have especially abused black and Black people with it. But it also has to be said that black intellectuals in America generally show the same lack of understanding of what race and racism are as white or other intellectuals. American culture has used race to block out what racism is, or to make it very difficult to understand what racism is, by projecting race so constantly and so forcefully. Black and white historians and other kinds of intellectuals among them, or other peoples in the United States, use the word "race." They talk of the "race factor." They say that it was "because of race," that Blacks were "denied" this or that or were "treated" a certain way because of their race, and other such expressions.

This is a heritage of the Enlightenment, and also the three and a half centuries of the black African slave trade and the centuries of exploiting black slave labor in the Western Hemisphere. All these things were locked together at the hip, in practice and in thought. In the case of the latter, it was racist thought. Contrary to what Saul Dubow said about the Enlightenment, or rather to add what he did not mention, Enlightenment thinkers were seeking to build a "natural" "history" and "natural" "world" and were using racist thought to construct them, the "natural" "history" of the white "race" and their "natural" "world," and the "natural" "history" of the black "race" and their "natural" "world." This all amounts to social construction, but it is the use of language to distort, misrepresent, and to falsify, to make fantasies stand for reality.

This was the broad task of the written racist narratives, which could appear in letters, diaries, memoirs, government documents, magazines, dramas, histories, books, or articles, and all forms were used over the centuries of the Enlightenment and the black African slave trade and the White use of black slave labor. These things, after all, were against what the Enlightenment stood for, what presumably European civilization stood for, what civilization stood for. But in fact, it was civilization—the "civilized world"—that was doing these things: enslaving people, killing people, maiming people, exploiting people, and in a myriad of ways abusing people, and by the millions. People of the Western world had to be made to believe that this was all right or all necessary, and that there was nothing wrong, illegal, or immoral about it. But more so, that all that was happening was what nature demanded, and even what God wanted or intended. These projections could not have been done by simply propagating racist beliefs. This required continuous long or short written racist accounts, and, of course, the continuous application of racist power, power exercised on the assumption that people were not people or full human beings. The social construction that went on in all these media of presentation and delivery was not about race, but about "race."

The Enlightenment thinkers socially constructed race to produce "race," a falsification and even a denial of the former, since "race" was an invisibilization of race. But the black race, in fact, was not invisibilized and could not be, not living among white people. So white people had to be convinced that what they saw was not what they saw. This kind of convincing had to be strong and comprehensive, and continuous. That meant that "race" had to be continuously constructed and presented to a public that had to be made to believe. None of this was rational. It was irrational, but it was *logical* behavior.

Enlightenment thought was based on the metaphysical philosophical premise that human beings were rational in their nature. This was a belief, not a fact; one of those absolute truths that the Enlightenment philosophers could not verify empirically. What they could have verified empirically was that human beings, as human beings, because of their brains and cognitive capabilities, and thus on the basis of what was inherent in and natural to them, sought to be logical in their thinking. They had the potential to be rational, but they also had the potential to be irrational. When they were either of these things, they sought to be logical in their thinking and expressions, to give coherence, structure, and even stability. An empirical truth is that being logical is not necessarily the same as being rational or engaging in rationality. Theologians of the European Middle Ages, and centuries afterward to the eighteenth century, employed reason and philosophy to bolster and to attempt to verify their irrational religious beliefs. The philosophers and others of the Enlightenment used logical reasoning socially to construct "race." In short, logical reasoning was reflected in the construction of their white supremacist/ebonicistic racist beliefs, as well as their maleist/sexist beliefs.

When theologians engage in this kind of activity it has been labeled *scholasticism* by historians and philosophers. When philosophers or other kinds of thinkers use racist beliefs to undergird their thoughts, or when scientists used them, as Enlightenment scientists did, these were manifestations of *racist scholasticism*. Western social science that became academic and professional in the later stages of the Enlightenment, in the late nineteenth and early twentieth centuries, was inundated with racism as foundational thinking and in the construction of social science. These were the years of the so-called "scientific racism." This is a nonsensical term, because science cannot verify racist fantasies or the existence of "race" or "races," although it can verify the existence of race and races.

A legacy of the Enlightenment of the eighteenth century and also of the black African slave trade and black slavery was the belief on the part of people that black Africans and black or Black people were slaves or were made slaves because of their race. This is common thinking among Black and white historians. Race was never the reason for the enslavement of black people or the myriad of ways that white people exploited or abused black or Black people. Cornel West titled one of his books *Race Matters*, which conveyed the view that Black people did what they did in America, or responded to Whites in the country, because of their race, and that Whites related to Blacks the way they did because of their race.[25] Frederick Douglass made the observation back in the nineteenth century that the race of black people was not the reason they were made slaves, or why they were continually mistreated by Whites even when they were nonslaves. In a piece for his own newspaper, the *North Star*, he wrote,

Color is not the cause of our persecution; that is, it *is not our color* which makes our proximity to white men disagreeable. The evil lies deeper than prejudice against color. It is, as we have said, an intense hatred of the colored man when he is distinguished for any ennobling qualities of head and heart. If the feeling which persecutes us were prejudice against color, the colored servant would be as obnoxious as the colored gentleman, for the color is the same in both cases; and being the *same* in both cases, it would produce the *same* result in both cases.[26]

In my book *Racism Matters*, I showed that race was a secondary matter with white people. It was the vehicle or means through which they expressed their racist views toward Blacks and engaged in racist behavior toward them on the white supremacist/ebonicistic racist assumption that they were of a "race" of "godly" or "godlike" "entities," and Black people were of a "race" of "nonhumans" or "subhumans."

For Enlightenment and other thinkers white supremacy/ebonicism became the means to rationalize and justify the black African slave trade and black slavery, and reasoning logic could be used to present these things to make them palpable to themselves and others.[27]

Owing to white supremacist/ebonicistic thinking, black people were not human beings or were not full human beings. Thus, human or divine morality did not apply to them, and others did not have to be restrained by such restrictions when relating to black people. If black people were not human nor fully human, they did not have much cerebral capability or even moral capability. They were more like passive objects or things, or inanimate objects. Like other things, they could be considered property, and like other property could be legally owned. Indeed, given their great innate inferiority, and thus their inability really to care for themselves, or even to develop substantially, slavery fitted them and was commensurate with their innate and stable low-quality attributes. Slavery could be understood as the natural condition of black people, and white people stood naturally as their masters or overlords.

Enlightenment thinkers constructed racist narratives that mainly emphasized race, but were at all times mainly about "race": a cluster of fantasies about who black people were and what they were or were not capable of doing, and the inherent right of white people to treat them according to their "nature." The narratives were presented logically, but were predicated on an irrational premise and reflected the use of logic to try to verify irrational beliefs; that is, using logic to carry illogical beliefs and thinking to their logical conclusion. In America, racism and white supremacy/ebonicism were welded so tightly to race and slavery, and thus to black and Black people, that white people, generation after generation, associated the black race and Black people with slavery, and were taught and concluded that black and Black people were slaves because of their race. From there they were taught and concluded that the race of black people or Blacks was their weakness, was evidence of their inferiority, and would always be a barrier between them and white people, and would require white people to treat them on the basis of their race.

But all the while, white people treated black and Black people on the basis of their racist views that were constructed from the racial feature of such people, which they invested with fantasies that produced the black "race," which was then imposed on black and Black people as their "inherent" or "natural" "attributes." White people related to black people as slaves in racist terms, and they related to nonslave black people in racist terms. Black people were made slaves not because they were black, but because white people, for their reasons, which included their racist reasons and their economic and political reasons, which were saturated with white supremacy/ebonicism, made them slaves and kept them as slaves. White people mistreated black or Black people because they were taught, one way or another, to do so, that it was their right to do so, and because their racist thinking, beliefs, psychology, and pathology compelled them to do so. In this mold of mind and psychology, white people were incapable of looking at black or Black people, or had great difficulty looking at such people, as being human beings and acting as human beings, and were often outraged when such people tried to act as human beings. This prompted many white people to vulgarity or violence, because black or Black people trying to act as human beings was offensive to their racist sensibilities and even a threat to their intellectual and psychological stability. Keeping Blacks slaves, suppressing Blacks, and abusing Blacks became means to maintain White inner peace and emotional and psychological stability.

One of the great delusions of white people over their history in America has been their belief that they have not been affected or affected seriously, intellectually, psychologically, morally, or spiritually, or that American history or American society have not been affected or affected seriously by their being racists, by holding Blacks in slavery for centuries, and by being cruel toward them in racist terms for centuries. Black historian Nathan Huggins attributed considerable blame to white historians for this delusional thinking on the part of Whites by the way they presented American history to them. In *Black Odyssey*, he wrote,

Slavery has been seen as a pathological condition, studied as a disorder which has consequences leading to the Civil War. At most, it was the Old South's particular pathology to be ultimately excised for the health of the nation. Racism and racial caste—which issue from racial slavery—have been, in their turn, studied as the "tangle of pathology" of blacks and the so-called underclass. Very little thought has been given to the general health of the society that created and sustains them. Society and its historians have treated all these phenomena as aberrations, marginal to the main story, to be quarantined if we extend the metaphor. Thus, our national history has continued to amplify the myths of automatic progress, universal freedom, and the American Dream without the ugly reality of racism seriously challenging the faith.[28]

The criticisms that Huggins extended to white historians he could have just as easily extended to Black historians, with the criticisms being slightly different. Black historians have shown almost no interest in writing about *American* history. They have left that task to white historians, and mainly white male historians, who usually write that kind of history. Thus, white historians can, as they do, downplay white supremacy/ebonicism and other racisms in American history and their impact on that history and American life. By their refusal to enter into that kind of writing, Black historians abet it, and also the continued promotion of White racisms in America through historical writing. But Black historians also do this by the way that they usually write on Black slavery in America. In 1972 John Blassingame published *The Slave Community* and made the astounding assertion that the work experience was not a major or meaningful experience for Black slaves.[29] That was the experience of the slave quarters and what happened there, the cultural and social things that Blacks did there. Black slaves worked about eighteen hours a day, most days of the week, each month, each year, and generationally. This could only be a major and meaningful experience for them and have a great impact on the way they functioned as slaves, and even on their motivation to engage in cultural and social construction. Blassingame presented an essentially idyllic view of Black plantation slavery in the American South, which he did by ignoring or downplaying the dictatorial, oppressive character of the institution and concentrating on the culture and social life that slaves developed.

Black historian after Black historian after 1972, with some white historians joining in, published studies of Black antebellum slavery that ignored or played down the dictatorial and oppressive character of the slavery, and that emphasized Black culture and Black social life significantly apart from white masters and the institution of slavery itself. This kind of writing on Black chattel slavery led historian Laurence Shore to make the following critical remarks: "For all their attention to Southern slave society, most historians have not created a tragic representation of the slave experience; they have sought to engender in their readers a catharsis of the tragic emotions—pity and fear. Struggle, defeat, isolation are not in the foreground of these historians' writing."[30]

Oppression, cultural and social construction, and tragedy are all a part of the Black slave experience in America. And that experience represents the great tragedy of America, to which Whites and Blacks are intimately connected. This would be seen when the Black slave experience was thoroughly integrated into the writing of American history, interpreting it on the basis of this included material, which would entail the requirement of interpreting Black slavery as inundated by racist beliefs, thinking, pathology, and social implementation. White historians have been loath to undertake this assignment, and this is also true of Black historians, who have simply shown little to no interest in writing on the subject of the larger American history. But if either kind of historian were to undertake the task, they would have to know the subject and reality of racism a lot better than they do, and employ a racist analysis in a critical manner throughout the length of the writing. It has always, since the late seventeenth and early eighteenth centuries, been racism, namely white supremacy/ebonicism, that has mattered to white Americans, and that has been central to American history, not race or the race factor or the racial factor. Always the *racist factor*.

Chapter 3

"Of Mr. Booker T. Washington and Others"

In *The Souls of Black Folk*, W.E.B. Du Bois titled the third chapter, "Of Mr. Booker T. Washington and Others." It was the most important essay in his book and it took on a measure of public importance. Du Bois offered some praise for Washington as a leader and for his efforts to help Black people in the South (which was most Black people in the country), but his writing was mainly critical of both of these things and signaled Du Bois's break with the Tuskegean. The criticism and break launched what was dubbed at the time, and for many decades afterward, the "Washington–Du Bois Controversy."

That controversy, nearly a hundred years old, still generates excitement, scholarship, and commentary among Black historians and other kinds of black intellectuals in America. What is to be said about most of the written efforts and commentary, however, is that both are rather superficial, one-sided, and uncritically in favor of Du Bois against the Tuskegean. There are three primary reasons why this general posture has prevailed. The first has to do with the two images that exercise considerable control on the writing on this subject: the image of Du Bois as an intellectual, a progressive thinker, and as a radical; and the image of Washington as pedestrian, conservative, and as an accommodationist. Moral and political value has been attached to these images, which has also guided scholarship or commentary, to the benefit of Du Bois and the disparagement of the Tuskegean.

The second primary reason for the prevailing view is that scholars and others have simply relied too much on Du Bois's interpretation of his conflict with Washington. This includes accepting the "radical" and "conservative" images, which Du Bois did much to construct and to pass on in numerous writings. Du Bois and others always exaggerated how large and significant this conflict was, which occurred mainly among elites among Blacks, with the mass of Black people being impervious to it.

The third primary reason for the continuing dominant view is the failure (or refusal) of most Black historians to deal in a full and realistic manner with Booker T. Washington. This failure extends to ignoring or making only the scantiest use of the *Washington Papers*, published in thirteen volumes. Fortunately, there have been some historians and other scholars over the years who have deviated from this sterile posture and sought to be more revelatory with respect to Washington, as to who he was, the kind of leadership he provided Black people, and his conflict with his Black adversaries. I have drawn on these scholars to devise my own historiographical stance on Washington and these other matters. I present it in this chapter. This chapter differs from others in this book, but it nevertheless fits in, because it presents a "critical reflection" on a manifestation of Black history, in this case my own, and also because it exhibits the criteria of "critical reflection" of all the chapters with respect to scholarship or commentary, analysis, and use of language.

Du Bois, hesitatingly at first and then with great enthusiasm, took up his leadership of the anti-Washington opposition, or the "anti-Bookerites" as they were sometimes called. Du Bois called such people, borrowing the concept from the Episcopal bishop the Reverend Alexander Crummell, the "Talented Tenth." There were people in this group who did not stay in alignment with Du Bois. Mary Church Terrell started out with Du Bois against Washington, then joined forces with the Tuskegean when she saw what he had achieved with his school in Tuskegee, Alabama. She then slid partly back into the Du Bois column with the launching of the Niagara Movement, but ultimately broke with Du Bois in 1910 over a matter associated with the newly established National Association for the Advancement of Colored People. William Ferris, a respectable Black intellectual initially opposed Washington, and was insulting about it. But two years into the Niagara Movement, in which he participated, he broke with Du Bois and the northern

Black opposition and became a Washington supporter. He wrote a letter to Washington, saying, "While I do not always agree with everything you say I believe that the greatness of your work and the grandeur of your achievement, and your grasp of the industrial condition in the South entitles you to rank with the great constructive geniuses of the century."[1]

Three things are to be noted here. Ferris regarded Washington's work among Blacks in the South as "great." He described the Grand Black Leader as a genius. He also praised him for his "grasp of the industrial condition in the South." In the 1930s Du Bois would be emphatic in saying that Washington did not understand the industrial transformation that was occurring in America during his life. Many Black and white historians have echoed this view. The view is not only erroneous, but is nonsensical. Washington spent a great deal of time with some of the people who were transforming America economically, and who were even transforming the South, in a lesser way, who were some of his principal financial supporters and political backers. Washington not only knew about the industrial and commercial transformation that was occurring in America, he was equally aware of the development in organization that was helping to facilitate it, and tried to pass this understanding on to the Black middle class and other Black people in America:

White men who deal in land are organized. White men who grow grain are organized. Those who grow peaches are organized. Those who grow apples are organized. Those who mine coal and iron are organized. Those who manufacture shoes are organized. Those who make dresses are organized. Those who make hats are organized. Those who sell groceries are organized. Those who are bankers are organized. Those who work in tin, lead, copper and wood are organized. If we Negroes would increase our business strength and influence, we must organize. Organize, organize, locally in the state and nation. Work together and stick together.[2]

As seen by his remarks, Washington fully understood that industrial and commercial specialization that functioned on an organized basis made for economic development and was helping to transform the American economy. White people were the models for this, and Washington had no compunction in trying to get Black industrialists and commercial elements to emulate them. So, clearly, to say that Washington did not know what was happening in America economically in his day is fatuous. When Du Bois made his negative comments about Washington along this line in the 1930s, he was himself under strong attack from Black leaders and Black intellectuals for the political and economic views he was espousing. He was criticized and condemned by individuals for being a socialist. There was objection to his socialist economic proposal for Black people, which was for them to establish economic cooperatives and to try to engage in economic development on that basis. Walter White, the executive director of the NAACP, sociologist E. Franklin Frazier, and economist Abraham Harris expressed great objection to this. They and other Blacks criticized what they regarded as Du Bois's call for "self-segregation" by Blacks to promote this economic adventure. Many critics accused Du Bois of being like Booker T. Washington, which led him to chop on the Alabamian, long since deceased, to take that kind of heat from himself. But that did not help, nor his effort to try to explain his new program that he wanted Blacks to undertake. He was forced to retire from the NAACP in 1934 and also lost control over and access to the monthly of the Association, *The Crisis*, that he had edited for twenty-five years. But what he had to say about his new proposal in that organ is important to repeat here. In 1934, in the monthly, he remarked,

Some people seem to think that the fight against segregation consists merely of one damned protest after another. . . . It is an undignified and impossible attitude and method to maintain indefinitely. Let us, therefore, remember that this program must be modified by adding to it a positive side. Make the Protest and keep on making it . . . but at the same time go to work to prepare methods and institutions which will supply those things and opportunities which we lack because of segregation.[3]

Du Bois also wrote in *The Crisis* in 1934,

Moreover, and beyond this I fight Segregation with Segregation, and I do not consider this compromise; I consider this common sense. . . . It's because I have enough sense to know . . . that either we get a segregated development here, or we get none at all; and the advantage of decent homes for five thousand colored people, outweighs any disadvantage which will come without this development.[4]

When Washington talked like this, in general terms, when he was the Grand Black Leader between 1895 and 1915, he was criticized by Du Bois and others of his essentially northern Black opposition as being "conservative," an "accommodationist," or an "Uncle Tom." Washington regarded his political, economic, and social programs for Blacks as expressions of "common sense." And decades before Du Bois made his proposal to combine public protest with socioeconomic construction, Washington had done it, making this proposal before the Afro-American Council, an organization that was trying to be essentially a Black protest vehicle. At the annual meeting in 1903, Washington said in an address,

In this connection we should bear in mind that our ability and our progress will be measured largely by evidences of tangible, visible worth. We have a right in a conservative and sensible manner to enter our complaints, but we will make a fatal error if we yield to the temptation of believing that mere opposition to our wrongs, and the simple utterance of complaint, will take the place of progressive, constructive action, which must constitute the bedrock of all true civilization. . . . Back of all complaint, all denunciation, must be evidences of character and economic foundation. An inch of progress is worth more than a yard of complaint.[5]

Du Bois's comments in the 1930s were shades of Washington, and also of what Washington did the following year. With Du Bois, he convened a conference at Carnegie Hall in New York City of oppositional elements to try to draw them around a program of combining public protest with Black cultural and social construction. Du Bois attended the conference for the purpose of sabotaging it, and he appealed to his supporters and hoped they would help him do that. He was very surprised when people he thought he would be able to count on to discredit Washington and the conference readily accepted the compromised program. Du Bois accepted it also, but only because he did not want to appear that he was a simple obstructionist. David Levering Lewis wrote in *W.E.B. Du Bois*, "Du Bois must have left the Carnegie Hall with a far clearer sense of his own limitations within a group setting as well as of the inevitability of conflict with Tuskegee."[6] He also left the meeting with the sense if not understanding that he could well have difficulties with people who could be his supporters, who sometimes found him hard to relate to and work with precisely because he found it difficult to compromise.

Du Bois actually broke with the Carnegie Compromise and Washington at the end of that spring, and received criticism from some people who stayed on; namely, Kelly Miller and Francis Grimke, people he had hoped would help him sabotage the Carnegie meeting. He fired criticism back at these men. "I count it a clear misfortune of the Negro race when two clear-headed and honest men like you can see their way to put themselves under the dictation of a man with the record of Mr. Washington. I am sorry, very sorry to see it. Yet it will not alter my determination one jot or tittle."[7] James Weldon Johnson, the first Black executive director of the NAACP after three previous white ones, who became Du Bois's friend and knew him well, wrote the following about him:

Du Bois in battle is a stern, bitter, relentless fighter . . . but his lack of the ability to unbend in his relations with people outside the small circle has gained him the reputation of being cold, stiff, supercilious, and has been a cause of criticism amongst even his adherents. This disposition, due perhaps to an inhibition of spontaneous impulse, has limited his scope of leadership.[8]

Du Bois showed conformity to this assessment when he acknowledged to Oswald Villiard in 1905, the white liberal publisher of *The Nation*, that Washington's "attitude on the race question is changing for the better," but that it still did not satisfy him.[9]

I have presented some facts and images of Booker T. Washington and W.E.B. Du Bois, based on the facts. Black historians especially, but also many white historians who write on the Tuskegean separately or in his relationship with Du Bois, usually ignore facts or evidence or make only meager use of them. Indeed, to say that they write on Washington is really overstating the case, because what they usually do is just make comments about him, and also, usually, just comments about him and his interaction with Du Bois. Most Black historians loath to think about Washington, let alone research, study, and write on him. The comments they make are usually the same, indicating how they copy each other in making them. John Brown Childs was different in what he had to say about Washington in *Leadership, Conflict, and Cooperation in Afro-American Social Thought*, and depicted him as an aggressive and thorough modernization leader.[10] Robert Franklin saw him as a social thinker in *Liberating Visions*.[11] Neither of these individuals was a historian; the former was a sociologist and the latter a religious scholar. One would think that Black historians who think of themselves as Black nationalist historians would fly to research the extant record on Washington, which is vast and published, and which reveals how he tried to help the mass of Black people develop in America and the way he tried to build a strong Black collectivity. But they show an unwillingness to do so.

When it comes to Washington and Du Bois, singly or together in interaction, such historians and others wish to view each or both from their own self-image and values, or from political values that they subscribe to or find attractive. Those values are "liberal," "progressive," "radical," or even "revolutionary." They, as they see it, can draw Du Bois under those concepts and images, but not Washington, and have others to spread over him: "conservative," "accommodationist," "reactionary," and "Uncle Tom." Black historians and other scholars have thrown an incredible obscurity and silence over Booker T. Washington, who in my view, and I feel reams of evidence shows, was a genius, known in his day as the "Wizard." The evidence shows that he understood power in a way that few Americans have ever understood it, and one would have to go to presidents, or governors, or powerful corporation heads to see his understanding duplicated. And Washington, as even some of his worst contemporary enemies had to admit, was a very adept leader, which even some of his detractors among historians have had to admit. One of them was Louis Harlan, who said the following about his leadership in the second volume of his biography of him: "His skill of maneuver and ability to make the most of bad circumstances—was his strong point as a leader."[12] Kelly Miller said the following about Washington's leadership: "The only Negro who has been able to force upon the acceptance of the American people a policy and program for his race. From this point of view he may be denominated the one commanding race statesman yet to appear."[13] Miller knew about Frederick Douglass, and even knew him personally, but his accolade did not go to him, nor did it go to Du Bois, whom he also knew and even worked with as a leader himself. And it was none other than Du Bois himself who acknowledged the gargantuan and adept character of Booker T. Washington's leadership. In his chapter "Of Mr. Booker T. Washington and Others," he said,

Then came the new leader. Nearly all the former ones had become leaders by the silent suffrage of their fellows, had sought to lead their own people alone, and were usually, save Douglass, little known outside their race. But Booker T. Washington arose as essentially the leader not of one race but of two— a compromiser between the South, the North, and the Negro.[14]

Washington was a leader of northern white people and southern white people and also Black people, a national leader of a group of people, and he led all these elements for twenty years. No one has ever been in such a powerful leadership position in American history that long. Du Bois reiterated these views about Booker T. Washington in his autobiography *Dusk of Dawn*, saying emphatically there, with respect to Black people, "There was no question of Booker T. Washington's undisputed leadership of ten million Negroes in America."[15] Of course, the leadership was disputed, principally by some northern Black opposition. But Du Bois did not suppress his understanding of how large and formidable Washington's leadership was with respect to Black people, and what he and other opposing elements were up against taking on Washington. When the Tuskegean's powerful white benefactors and supporters are added to the equation, who could frequently be persuaded to act as he wished them to, one can see clearly the enormity of his leadership and the great difficulty his opposition was up against.

Washington's powerful white benefactors did not want to attend the Carnegie Hall Conference in 1904. He persuaded some to attend, because he wanted to show his Black opposition how powerful he was, what his resources were, and why it was worthwhile to enter into compromise with him and his forces, and because he wanted his benefactors to endorse the compromised approach. Du Bois was furious at Washington's demonstration of strength. He resented the Tuskegean's powerful white supporters speaking at the conference, and all favorable toward the Alabamian. Du Bois lamented in his posthumously published *Autobiography*, "Even if all they said had been true, it was a wrong note to strike in a conference of conciliation."[16] But Du Bois had gone to the conference to try to wreck it before he knew some of Washington's benefactors and supporters would be there.

Du Bois has been able to draw Black historians and many white historians to his side, who go there because they do not significantly, let alone extensively, research and study this matter. They are attracted by Du Bois's own self-image as a "fighter" or "radical," which seems to concur with their own kind of thinking. They have also been drawn to the bigger-than-life image that Du Bois often presented of himself in his writings, which he was able to do by wrapping himself up in history, and in an image of history that was progressive and transformative; and, of course, by painting Washington as an obstacle to that history being realized. He has also been successful in getting historians and others to accept as real his exaggerated depiction of the struggle between Washington and his northern Black opposition. He often interpreted that struggle as if it were just between himself and Washington, with himself the good guy and on the side of progressive history and Washington the villain, trying to hold that history back. Here's what Du Bois said in *Dusk of Dawn*: "Since the controversy between myself and Mr. Washington has become historic, it deserves more careful statement than it has had hitherto, both as to matters and the motives involved."[17] He also remarked, "The fight cut deep: It went into social relations; divided friends; it made bitter enemies."[18] This last comment gives the impression that the 10 million Black people who lived in the country when this conflict opened up between 1903 and 1905 were divided equally between Washington and his opposition. Even James Weldon Johnson exaggerated this struggle:

It was the Niagara Movement, inaugurated by Dr. Du Bois in 1905, that marked, with respect to the question of the Negro's civil rights, a split of the race into two well-defined parties—one, made up from the preponderating number of conservatives, under the leadership of Booker T. Washington and the other, made up from the militant elements, under the leadership of W. E. B. Du Bois. Between these two groups there were incessant attacks and counter-attacks; the former declaring that the latter were visionaries, doctrinaires, and incendaries; the latter charging the former with minifying political and civil rights, with encouraging opposition to higher training and higher opportunities for Negro youth, with giving sanction to certain prejudiced practices and attitudes toward the Negro, thus yielding up in fundamental principles more than could be balanced by any immediate gains.[19]

It has to be remembered that Du Bois said in his autobiography that Washington was the undisputed leader of the 10 million Blacks in the country. Even allowing for the excessiveness of the comment, it certainly makes it implausible that Black people were equally split between followers of Washington and followers of Du Bois. Most Black people were southern Blacks, living in the rural South, and up against a vicious White racism, and were also poor and had no government looking out for their interests. Such Blacks, as the historical record clearly shows, were not engaged in a headstrong public battle in the South for political and civil rights, and they did not participate in the battle that went on between Washington and his northern Black opposition. The way Johnson described that battle, it is obvious that it was carried on by a limited number of Black people, mainly intellectuals and leaders. There has even been a prominent view that Black intellectuals were against Washington and on the side of the "radicals." But that notion was dispelled in 1963 by August Meier in *Negro Thought in America, 1880–1915*:

In reviewing the data we have presented on the thinking of an illustrative sampling of Negro intellectuals, it is evident that most of them—even those with a college education—were at one time or another (if not all the time) either enthusiastic or luke-warm supporters of Booker T. Washington, and that doctrines of racial pride, economics, solidarity, and self-help loomed large in their thinking, though of course their goal was full citizenship rights.[20]

Nell Irvin Painter put a peculiar interpretation on this Black political struggle. She denied that there was any struggle: "Most blacks found it possible simultaneously to accept Washington's South-centered practicality and Du Bois's insistence on full civil rights."[21] Most Black people lived in the South and were not, as said, protesting for political and civil rights. Moreover, most Blacks never even heard of Du Bois. They, of course, knew of Booker T. Washington and regarded him as their overarching leader. There was no way for Du Bois to be an equal competitor with Washington within Black America. At all times, from 1903–1905 on, he was a fiery individual and oppositional figure, but he had only a meager following and virtually no clout against the Tuskegean. Du Bois could never keep the firm support of many of his own followers. His importance came from his public protests and his political and other writings.

It is necessary to see very clearly how popular a leader Washington was among Black people in the United States, of which most Black or white historians seem not to have an inkling. His popularity was great in the North, which many a historian has denied, usually asserting how the adversary Niagara Movement cut into and diminished it, which was followed by the establishment of the NAACP, which really smashed it low. These are false images that show a glaring disregard for facts or evidence. The Niagara Movement lasted three years. It was always an elitist movement and never sought mass Black support, and thus had no significant following among Black people, not even in the North. Du Bois, Monroe Trotter, and other leaders of the Movement were constantly at each other. This made it vulnerable to Washington's actions against it. By 1907 the Movement was a paper reality and collapsed in 1908. It made no dent in Washington's armor or image. He was very popular among Blacks in the North during the entire existence of the Niagara Movement. In 1908, the year the Movement died, this is what a Black Cleveland newspaper editor wrote in his paper:

Washington is the saner course and more productive of substantial results. Du Bois gives us the ideal. His is the life of faith, he is always looking forward through a sad, cheerless veil. . . . Washington lifts the veil, lets the sunshine in and says "Today is the day of salvation; Drop your bucket where you are, wherever you happen to be." You can see the kind of program Washington advocates. Du Bois compensates us in "sweet dreams."[22]

In 1910 the NAACP was established. According to David Levering Lewis in *W.E.B. Du Bois* and following the traditional commentary on the situation, the establishment of the Association was the death knell of Washington's power and leadership over Black Americans. The evidence, which this assertion ignores, points to a directly opposite view. In 1910 Washington returned from a trip to England where he was feated by the monarchy, aristocrats, and large numbers of people. His first stop back in America was Boston, and then he made a tour of New England, making speeches, attending functions, and being celebrated. Boston was Monroe Trotter's home base, and the home base of other of the Tuskegean's critics. Black people in New England had been sprayed with this criticism for years. When Washington returned to Boston following his tour of New England the following occurred, as reported by a local newspaper:

Returning to Boston Tuesday evening Dr. Washington found at the depot an automobile which had been provided by the United Committee of Colored Elks, which conveyed him to Paine Memorial Hall on Appleton Street, where a reception and band concert were being held at the Elks. Some seven or eight hundred ladies and gentlemen were present. They welcomed the Negro leader with cheers, handclapping, the waving of handkerchiefs, etc., and gave every evidence of sincere pleasure in being able to entertain him as a guest of the occasion. . . . Negro Boston, as represented by these seven or eight hundred ladies and gentlemen, was certainly responsive to the occasion and drowned with applause again and again the eloquent words of appreciation which fell from the lips of the recently returned traveller.[23]

At the turn of the century, Washington had been told by some Black leaders in Boston, at a gathering at which he spoke, to return to the South and let leaders like themselves take care of the political destiny of Blacks in the country. In 1905 he was heckled during a speech in Boston. In 1910, as just seen, he was the man of the hour among the educated and affluent Black people of the city, as represented by the people attending the occasion, which included what Du Bois would have called elements of the "Talented Tenth." This situation was duplicated in other places that Washington toured in New England.

But it was in the South that Washington exercised his leadership of Blacks most powerfully and successfully, and where he was virtually worshipped by the Black population. Historians who side with Washington's opposition always convey the impression that a reference to Black people was a reference to Black people of the North, totally ignoring the Black people of the South, where nine-tenths of the Black population resided. Whenever it is said that Du Bois and others like him led Black people this is utterly false. Most Black people in the South did not know Du Bois or any of the other people who claimed to speak for them, who claimed they were leading them, and who insisted on determining their destiny in the country. Washington was the leader of the Black people, the Grand Black Leader, for twenty years. He led Black people where most of them lived and where it was the most dangerous for Blacks to live in the country. But he would not leave it and leave the mass of Blacks there. He was their best protection, their best hope, and their greatest inspiration. This is shown in the accounts in the *Washington Papers*, edited by Louis Harlan and others, of his weeks-long or month-long tours of the South to talk to Black people, and also to gatherings of Black and white people. When Washington made speeches in the South, powerful white political officials, including governors, businessmen, educators, and other Whites, attended, and there were also Black politicians, businessmen, educators, and others at these gatherings. Washington always spoke to overflowing separate Black audiences. This occurred over the twenty years he was the Grand Black Leader. This meant that he was still exercising great power and leadership in the years following the establishment of the NAACP until his death in 1915. That year, Washington made a month-long tour of Louisiana, which was recorded in newspapers that showed the great reverence exhibited toward him, especially by Black people:

Meetings were held in New Orleans, St. Bernard Parish, New Iberia, Crowley, Lake Charles, Lafayette, Southern University, Baton Rouge, Alexandria, Gibsland, Shreveport, and Mansfield. Everywhere Mr. Washington and his party were met at railroad stations by crowds of black people; other crowds of white citizens gathered to see him and to hear him expound his gospel of industrial opportunity and racial good-will.

Negroes came on mule back, in carriages, and in wagons, long distances— ten, twenty, thirty, and even forty miles. They gathered in the thousands at railroad stations to see the "wizard of Tuskegee." They stood for hours to get a chance to hear the most distinguished member of their race tell them of progress and opportunities in the Southland. There were literally miles of people and vehicles. Good-natured policemen were sometimes nearly carried off their feet in the effort to keep a path open through the eager throngs, but there was no trace of disorder. Everyone was happy, sober, receptive.

Equally encouraging was the attitude of white people—men and women of distinction in southern life. Mayor Behrman of New Orleans said to Mr. Washington . . .

N. C. Blanchard of Shreveport, ex-governor of Louisiana said in introducing Mr. Washington to an audience of over 10,000 white and colored citizens. . . .[24]

This description of Washington and the great mass of Black and white people gathered around him in the state of Louisiana, which also occurred when he toured other states in the South in no way projects the images of psychopant, toady, accommodationist, cowerer, or "Uncle Tom" that Washington's northern Black opposition tried to paste on him, and that many present-day historians do hang on him, explicitly or by implication. The same realities completely contradict the image that Black and other historians and other kinds of scholars project, that say that the Tuskegean began to lose his power, charisma, prestige, and ability to lead Blacks when the NAACP was established.

The truth about the NAACP was that it was an organization that during the last five years of Washington's life was just barely staying alive, and was on the verge of collapsing in 1915. Many northern Blacks were suspicious of the organization and shunned it, such as Monroe Trotter and Ida-Wells Barnett. Du Bois was the only Black person on the organization's national board, and there was continued criticism in Black newspapers, in addition to the ones that Washington controlled and/or had great influence with, of the white leadership of the rights organization. There was always great conflict at the top of the Association between Du Bois and his white coleaders and coworkers. He reacted sharply to any display of racism, and it occurred often. There was also a running feud with Du Bois about *The Crisis*. This was the official organ of the NAACP, which Du Bois had founded as Director of Publications and Research of the institution. He considered the monthly magazine his own organ to express his own views about the racist/racial situation in America. There was objection to this monopoly, and also resentment that Du Bois did not usually say much that was positive about Whites or encouraging for them, as to what they might do to help. Mary White Ovington, one of the cofounders of the Association, a member of the national board, and Du Bois's friend, expressed her dissatisfaction at this exclusionary writing: "Now no one can be more persuasive than you before a white audience, or can write more persuasively to white people. But when you edit *The Crisis* that white audience is sometimes forgotten and its feelings are badly hurt, or feelings of resentment are aroused."[25]

Joel Spingarn, the second chairman of the Association, replacing Oswald Villiard, who went rounds with Du Bois, particularly about *The Crisis*, felt that the friction between Du Bois and the white members of the board, which was having ramifications in local organizations, was threatening the very existence of the Association. He expressed his great concern to Du Bois in a letter:

I agree with your critics that we cannot go on unless your talents are subordinated to the general welfare of the whole organization and the rift between the various departments of the Association is closing once and for all. . . . If you are not willing to espouse our cause wholeheartedly as one with your own, I am afraid that the Association is doomed.[26]

It was sliding down a slippery slope in 1915, heading for a crash at the bottom. The Association was forced to adopt "the policy of suspending branches because of lack of activity, their members being retained as members-at-large of the Association. In order to lessen the chance of new branches failing, another policy was adopted—that organizing groups would first receive recognition as provisional committees or 'locals,' which, if successful, would at the end of a year be chartered as branches."[27] May Childs Nerney, the white national secretary of the NAACP, resigned from the organization. She filed a report to it that offered a gloomy and perhaps even non-existent future. "She was pessimistic about the future of the NAACP because of the failure of either its program or *The Crisis* to reach the masses of colored people. The illiterate and lowly of the race 'do not speak our language,' she said." Mary White Ovington was to remark that the NAACP was "just one among many 'insignificant' reform groups housed in New York."[28] Finally, historian Eugene Levy, in 1973, talked of the great weakness of the NAACP in its early years: "Between 1910–1916 those who took an active role in the NAACP struggled, sometimes desperately, to create a viable organization. To remain in existence was the key problem of the earlier years."[29] But Robert Factor, in his book *The Black Response* in 1970, spoke of the strength of the NAACP and its threat to Washington's power and leadership. Louis Harlan did the same in the second volume of his biography of the leader. David Levering Lewis did the same, entitling a chapter in *W.E.B. Du Bois*, "Rise of the Crisis, Decline of the Wizard." Earlier political scientist John McCartney had expressed the historiographical line in his book *Black Power Ideologies*. He said Washington's general opposition

took on firm organizational form with the formation of the strongly political and integrationalist National Association for the Advancement of Colored People (NAACP), in 1910. The formation of the NAACP signified that Washington was rapidly losing his hold over the fortunes of the blacks in America, and indeed "by the time he died Washington had lost much of his power."[30]

The only thing that stopped Washington was his bad health and his death. The NAACP was never a match for him and the power he wielded (i.e., his Tuskegee Machine). Indeed, what Washington's detractors always leave out, because of their lack of research and study of the matter, is that the NAACP was able to exist initially precisely because he let it come into existence. He had the power to crush it, and that was what the white movers of the institution were afraid of. Mary White Ovington wrote,

I think it's legitimate now [many years later] to raise the curtain a little. Our controversy was a part of the time in which we lived and was inevitable. It centered about Booker T. Washington. Was it possible to build up any organization, to get support for what we knew would become expensive work, without his sanction? Must we not at least ask him to be on our committee. . . . Could we ignore the man who was unquestionably the most influential and the most famous Negro living.[31]

Washington had no interest in working with the white or Black movers who were trying to launch the new rights organization, because he wanted to remain independent of it and to keep an eye on it, to be able to move against it if he had to. But he was happy to see the new organization come into existence. It was a political and civil rights organization mainly, and would be fighting for Black political and civil rights in the American courts. This he had been doing secretly for years, which was difficult, time consuming, and expensive. He was glad to turn this activity over to other parties. What concerned him the most about the new organization was that the Whites who were establishing it and who would control it might try to use it to lead Black people in the country. He would crush it if it tried to do that, making itself his direct rival. It would have to go the way of the Niagara Movement.

Neither Black people nor white people from the North, at such a remote distance, would be permitted to lead Blacks in the South. But the idea of white people leading Black people alone galled Washington. As he wrote to his personal secretary and confidant, and also one of his emissaries, Emmett Jay Scott, "We welcome the assistance and advice of such disinterested men as Dr. Frissell, Mr. Ogden and others, but we are not ready to be taken charge of bag and baggage by any white man."[32] The Tuskegean wrote to Timothy Thomas Fortune with respect to this matter, and as it related directly to the NAACP: "We are having the old game played over again of white people trying to lead colored people. I am not, however, alarmed, as I have passed through many storms in the past."[33] Washington could have mobilized Black people against the NAACP on this issue alone, and on this basis alone could have brought it down. To get the NAACP established it was Washington who had to be accommodated. The Tuskegean had to be accommodated in order for Du Bois to be appointed Director of Publications and Research for the new organization. Washington made it clear to those determining the appointment that he was opposed to Du Bois getting it if he intended to use the position as a means to attack him publicly. Du Bois had to bite his tongue and agree that he wouldn't. In his autobiography, *Dusk of Dawn*, Du Bois tried to put the best face on his humiliation, an account he left out of the later *Autobiography*:

With some hesitation I was asked to come as Director of Publications and Research, with the idea that my research work [at Atlanta University, his Atlanta sociological studies] was to go on with the further idea that my activities would be so held in check that the Association would not develop an organ of attack upon Tuskegee—a difficult order; because how, in 1910, could one discuss the Negro problem and not touch upon Booker T. Washington and Tuskegee? But after all, as I interpreted the matter, it was a question of temperament and manner rather than of subject.[34]

It was more than a matter of temperament, which Du Bois did not convey in his remarks; namely, it was a matter of survival of the new organization, even its ability to get off the ground. Du Bois made the following comment in the *Autobiography*, that there was a "critical if not hostile public which expected the NAACP generally to launch a bitter attack upon Booker T. Washington and Tuskegee."[35] This was a false, self-serving comment, because there was no such public in 1910, Black or White. Washington was immensely popular with both groups at that time.

It should be obvious to anyone that with all the power, prestige, and leadership capabilities that Washington had, charges of him being weak of character, submissive, obsequious, or even an "Uncle Tom" would not fit him. Masses of Black and white people would not have put their fate in the hands of such a person and been that supportive and loyal, certainly not for two decades. But these were precisely the images that Louis Harlan projected of Washington in his award-winning two-volume biography. This biography was distinguished mainly by being an elaborate update of the traditional view of Washington as someone who did wrong by Black people. Harlan caricatured Washington's leadership by comparing it to an urban "political boss." No given urban political boss led white people and Black people nationally and regionally. He projected an image of Washington as being spineless, which came through in one of his remarks: "Somewhere back in his life the power to lose his temper with a white man had been schooled out of him."[36] He even conveyed the impression that Washington was a weasel. This was how he described Washington in his efforts to help Blacks fight against segregation and for political and civil rights: "He did these things more by private action than by ringing declaration. Most of his public utterances on civil rights contained weasel words."[37] Harlan's idea of "weasel words" were any words that were not biting, caustic, militant, confrontational, or belligerent. He praised Washington's northern Black opposition, the Niagara Movement and the NAACP, for using such words, and their aggressive public protest methods. But neither of these groups gained back for Blacks the national citizenship and national political and civil rights that had been taken from them in the early 1880s. And the Black opposition failed against Washington: the Niagara Movement went out of business, and the NAACP was on the verge of collapse in 1915.

Washington was helping Black people in the way he saw his leadership and programs having to help them: helping them develop as a people, culturally, socially, and economically. Harlan was not interested in this aspect of Washington's leadership. He even called it "wrongheaded," "ill-advised," and similar things. But how could helping a people just released from slavery modernize and develop be called "wrongheaded?" Harlan felt that Washington should have devoted himself and his leadership to helping Black people attain their full rights in America. Since he knew that that was not Washington's main interest in leading his massive constituency, he knew that his subject was vulnerable to criticism and he leveled it, going to the extreme of referring to Washington as being spineless, more or less. The following are some examples of the way Washington talked to white people, and very powerful white people, taken from the papers that Harlan and his associates edited.

In a letter to President Roosevelt, Washington wrote,

My dear Mr. President: I want to congratulate you heartily upon your address at Oyster Bay. I write, however, especially to say that I am glad that you did not touch upon the matter of the Southern question. Waiving for the moment the matter of right and justice, as a matter of political expediency, at this time in my opinion, it will be wise for you to make no reference to that subject in your formal letter of acceptance.[38]

In a letter to President William Howard Taft, Washington said,

My dear President Taft: . . . In the year 1913 the Negro race will have been free in this country fifty years. I have been asked by the National Negro Business League and other prominent organizations and individuals among our race to initiate a movement looking toward the celebration of this event by some kind of exposition. . . .

If the matter is taken up, I . . . have in mind . . . getting the Southern white people to take an interest in it and getting the two races to take an interest and part in the exposition. . . .

My special point in writing you just now is to suggest that you not commit yourself in any direction on this subject until I can have an opportunity of seeing you in person, which I shall try to do sometime after you have gotten back to Washington and have gotten some of your hard work off your hands.[39]

Washington wrote the following short letter to William Henry Baldwin, a railroad magnate, one of his principle benefactors and a prominent white man of his Tuskegee Machine:

I want to emphasize if possible what I suggested to you in our short conversation on Sunday night regarding Mr. Murphy. I find that he naturally is not very happy over present conditions. He is chafing under restraint and restrictions, etc. . . . The main point of this letter is to suggest that at some time you give him an opportunity to talk with you very frankly and freely about his condition; you will have to encourage him to do so.[40]

Finally, Washington's letter in 1903 to the white president of Berea College, William Goodell Frost, read,

I call your attention to a matter in which you are quoted in the enclosed clipping taken from the N.Y. Tribune of Feb 9. I dislike very much to see you quoted as stating that the white man should be educated before the Negro is educated. . . . I think it wholly unfair for anyone to make the statement that the white man should be educated first. . . . A broader and more statesmanlike thing would be to say that both races should be educated.[41]

Washington was a man of great power, prestige, and persuasive capabilities, and he did not have to be raucous or belligerent to get people to act or to get things done. But he saw no efficacy in that approach anyway. And it could be very dangerous for Black people in the South to employ it, when they had neither national, state, county, or local government to protect and help them, and when so many white people in the South did not hold their lives dear on any count. There had to be a different way to lead in this kind of context, and also when one's own constituency was just up from slavery, massively illiterate, poor, and accustomed, from centuries of slavery, of being dependent upon and obedient to all white people and doing as the latter commanded them. Having a definite program, being firm and persuasive, developing and displaying leadership skills, and getting followers to make tangible progress was Washington's view of how he and Blacks should proceed in the South.

And as the Tuskegean perfectly understood, he needed white people to help Black people in these efforts. Getting former masters to help took a certain skill, not bad talk or belligerency. The Czechoslovak President Vaclav Havel understood fully the kind of communication skills that Washington had to have trying to lead Blacks in the South:

It is largely a matter of form: knowing how long to speak, when to begin, and when to finish; how to say something politely that your opposite number may not want to hear; how to say, always, what is most significant at a given moment, and not to speak of what is not important or relevant; how to insist on your own position without offending; how to create the kind of friendly atmosphere that makes complex negotiations easier.[42]

Havel said he had to learn these communication skills as president of his country. At this height of power he said, "I have discovered that good taste is more useful here than a degree in political science."

In keeping with his interest to project the traditional view of Washington as an "Uncle Tom"—as an "Uncle Tom in his Own Cabin,"[43] which had been his characterization in an article published before he put out the first volume of his biography—Harlan not only decried Washington's program to help Blacks, he made it appear that Washington did not really have the intellectual acumen to fix on what was really indispensible to accomplish for Blacks:

Those who try to understand Washington in ideological terms, as the realistic black philosopher of the age of Jim Crow, or as the intellectual opposite of W. E. B. Du Bois, miss the essential character of the man. He was not an intellectual, but a man of action. Ideas he cared little for. Power was his game, and he used ideas simply as instruments to gain power.[44]

Harlan turned to Du Bois for support of this assertion, quoting Du Bois, who had said that Washington did not have "an abstraction about him." For the Tuskegean, "It wasn't a matter of ideals or anything of that sort."[45] Harlan did not seem to realize that trying to discredit Washington as an intellectual and his thought was about the only way that Du Bois could try to confront him. In his chapter, "Of Mr. Booker T. Washington and Others," Du Bois had remarked of Washington, "The picture of a lone black boy poring over a French grammar amid the weeds and dirt of a neglected home soon seemed to him the acme of absurdities. One wonders what Socrates and St. Francis of Assisi would say to this."[46] Washington might well have said that neither one of those men lived in the viciously racist South of the late nineteenth and early twentieth centuries, and he would also likely have said that he would have preferred to see a little Black boy and girl reading English grammars in a well-built and decent house. Washington was not a romantic or romantic thinker. He was a realist and a realistic thinker.

What was realistic and necessary for Blacks, he thought, was for them to modernize and develop as fast as they could. That required modernization and development ideas for Blacks to follow, and Washington developed them; indeed, a very elaborate theory of modernization and development could be culled from the Tuskegean's vast extant record if anyone was inclined to make the effort. In 1970 Robert Factor, in his book *The Black Response*, which Harlan cited as one of his contacted secondary sources, said the following about the Tuskegean:

It is one of the least appreciated facets of Washington's career and personality that he was highly theoretical insofar as a social theory may be regarded as a set of unproved assumptions which explain the isolated facts
of social experience and relates them to each other. . . . Washington added
to this delusion [that he was not an intellectual or theoretically inclined]
by denouncing abstract thought and thinkers and by emphasizing the practiced and concrete. But as theory is a working hypothesis and guide to
action, Washington was profoundly theoretical.[47]

Finally, Harlan reasserted the traditional view, as a reflection of
the "Uncle Tom" image, that Washington "sold-out" Black people
in his Atlanta Address of 1895, which Harlan called a "Faustian
Deal" in the first volume of his biography. In the second volume he
reasserted the traditional view that Washington was a failed leader
because of his "inability to reverse the hard times for blacks during
what whites called the Progressive Era. What was for Washington
personally the best of times was for most blacks the worst."[48]

Let's take the first of these matters for comment. The "Faustian
Deal" was made in 1877, when some northern and southern white
politicians made a deal to put Rutherford B. Hayes in the White
House in return for letting southern Whites have full control over
Black people and their ability to do with them as they wished without national government or northern interference. The Supreme
Court aided this deal in the early 1880s by declaring the Civil Rights
Act of 1875 unconstitutional and vitiating the Fourteenth and Fif-
teenth Amendments as they applied to Blacks, which took their
national citizenship away and their national political and civil
rights. It was only necessary for southern states to do their part,
which they did by passing state statutes to disenfranchise Blacks,
over decades, and which was a process that had begun and was
moving rapidly regionally before Washington made his Atlanta
Address. White people sold out Black people and America, but
Harlan could only blame Washington for all this, a Black victim.
But Black historians and other Black scholars have blamed Washington, and have also made him the victim. Political scientist/his-
torian Manning Marable viewed Washington as a "betrayer" of
Blacks.[49] Years earlier, historian Thomas Holt had described
Washington's leadership of Blacks in the South as "sterile and pu-
sillanimous."[50] That description would seem to have been more apropos of those Black individuals in the North who would not come
to the South to try to lead Blacks, but who sought to do so from the
great distance and greater safety of the North.

In his Atlanta Address Washington sought to keep Blacks closely
attached to the rich and powerful in America; namely, the new economic corporate giants, who were also the country's great philan-

thropists. Blacks were in desperate need of financial help. They needed what would be described today in developmental theory as "capital transfers." Washington proposed a deal of taking Blacks out of a public protest posture to pursue political and civil rights, saying agitation was "extremist folly," given the way the South was. He also accepted the social separation of Blacks, which he did not regard as much of a concession at all. Blacks were not seeking to mingle socially with Whites, and the latter were not seeking to mingle socially with Blacks. What Washington understood was that southern Whites associated social mingling between Blacks and Whites with sexual intercourse and marriage. It was White emotion and irrationality that Washington had to pare down, because it could lead to violence and the obstruction of efforts on the part of Blacks to modernize and develop in the South. In exchange for what Blacks would do, Washington wanted two things: northern and southen upper-class white men with wealth to help Blacks build schools and establish economic enterprises as motor powers to modernize and develop, and endorsement as the general leader of Black people.

It has always been wrong to say that white people *picked* Washington for this role. He was already the primary leader of Black people. Black people at this time meant southern Blacks, and Washington had been leading masses of them since 1881, when he began constructing the Tuskegee Institute. He was well-known among Black people in the South by 1895. His knowledge of that and feeling that he had the right program for the time, for Blacks, Whites in the South, and the South, and for northern Whites and the relations between the two sections of the country, induced him to seek endorsement of powerful men, because he wished to play a powerful role as a powerful leader. He was invited to make a speech at the Atlanta Exposition. He knew there would be powerful northern and southern white people in the audience, and that other such people around the country would learn about the speech. He came with a plan of action that he wanted to lead people in carrying out, and he got the endorsement he sought. James Weldon Johnson called the Atlanta Address "great." Du Bois said the following about it in a letter to Washington: "My Dear Mr. Washington: Let me congratulate you upon your phenomenal success at Atlanta—it was a word fitly spoken."[51]

As to Washington's ability to reverse the hard times for Blacks during the Progressive Era, this was not only something that he could not do, it was something that all the millions of Black people could not do, or they and their White allies. They might have been able to if they had had the national, state, county, and other American governments to help, but those institutions were helping to suppress Black people during the so-called Progressive Era. They might have been able to if the white philanthropists had been willing to make larger capital transfers. They might have been able to if white Americans had not become so acutely racist, and had not joined the Whites/Europeans in their determination to bring all people of dark hue on the planet under their domination, control, and exploitation. The Progressive Era was an Oppressive Era for Blacks. And they cannot be blamed for it. This is blame, as historical evidence shows, that has to be placed at the feet of white people, which Harlan, obviously, did not want to do.

As to the Progressive/Oppressive Era being a "best time" for Washington, one could only make that remark if they overlooked the planned and near-missed assassinations of Washington, or the fact that he had to deal with the knowledge of Black people being publicly humiliated daily by white people, and killed and brutalized by the thousands. It could only be a "best time" for him if one thought that he did not feel badly about or did not weep over so many millions of Black people being so poor and uneducated, and at the whims and mercy of people who thought of them as being "nonhumans" or "subhumans." Washington dedicated his life to helping Black people. He drove himself into poor health doing so, because he would not, as so many people close to him tried to get him to do, stop driving himself. He drove himself into an early grave at fifty-six. And all the years he had bad, even crippling health and still drove himself could not have been "personally the best times for him."

The Tuskegean also drove his Tuskegee Machine. This was a structure of people, alliances, and a multiplicity of institutions, political, economic, education, and other kinds, that were held together by Washington's dextrous use of power, his charismatic personality and leadership, and the ideology that threaded it, which Washington called the "Tuskegee Idea" (i.e., his racial ideals, such as racial pride, racial unity, and racial progress) and his modernization ideas and programs to help Blacks in America. The Machine was also held together by the desire on the part of its participants to be successful in their efforts. Washington exercised centralized power through the Machine, but he also, at the same time, encouraged local manifestations of the Machine to take local initiative. The major part of the Tuskegee Machine was the Tuskegee Institute and the thousands of young Black leaders that Washington persuaded to go into the rural areas of the South from the Tuskegee Institute and other Black educational institutions where he had great influence. It was only through persuasion that he could get Black youth to go into the rural areas, because he did not have the power to compel them. But over decades he persuaded thousands of them to do so, which meant young Blacks going into the most racist and violent areas of the South to lead Blacks. The Tuskegean's injunction to these youthful leaders, who in modernization theory of a later date would be called "cadres," was direct, firm, and messianic:

When you go out to work, stop where the people need your help the most, where you can accomplish the most good, go not in the place where you are to be most pleasantly located, find the corner that is the darkest where the people have the least help and see how bright and cheerful you can make them.[52]

He also said to them that for them to make their leadership immediate, communicable, and effective with the people, they had to "talk simply to them. Don't use any big words and high flown sentences. Don t go out to show your education; talk to them in plain, simple words. Simply have the people sit down and talk to them in a plain common-sense way."[54] He also said to his young helpers, "If you have anything to write, write it in the plainest manner possible. Use just as few words as possible. If you get a word with one syllable that will express your meaning, use it in preference of two syllables. . . . Try to get one or two syllables instead of three or four. . . . There is great power in simplicity of speech."[54]

The young Black leaders would be moving among masses of illiterate and semi-illiterate Black people. Language had to draw them in, not keep them out. The use of language with modernization and development was a theoretical conception with Washington, because it could expedite or hinder them. Historians have often spoken of how Washington was "pedestrian" in his own writing and speaking, and often compared him unfavorably to some of his northern Black opposition, who were college or university educated. But Washington knew who his social constituency was and where they had come from, and figured out the best way to use langauge with them and passed this understanding onto his young leaders.

Washington kept in touch with his youthful cadres by corresponding with them. When they wrote to him, he would publish some of the letters in a Tuskegee organ, *The Southern Letter*, and then distribute the letters and the remarks widely throughout the South to try to draw other Black youth to his ranks as new members of the Tuskegee Machine. The Tuskegean also visited his youthful cadres when he made his tours of the South. An example of what one of these individuals would write to Washington was what one said in

1888: "I am putting forth every effort to bring these people out of darkness into light. They say they are going to give me a three months independent school after this term is out. So I will have about a six months school."[55] Another cadre remarked, "I have an enrollment of 72 pupils. My work is hard yet I do not mind it. I believe I could go into any dark corner of the State and be satisfied, for I know and feel it to be my duty to help my race."[56] Another young leader reported, "On the whole I can see a great improvement in the condition of the people since I have been teaching here. Not so many mortgage their crops . . . as has been the case before. They seem more saving and depend more on themselves. They take more interest in sending their children to school regularly every day."[57]

At a later time, after Washington had established annual leadership conferences at the Tuskegee Institute, which saw his young leaders establish local ones that were all part of the Tuskegee Machine, one of the young leaders reported, "In this Conference we held I found that better homes, schools and churches were being built by our race. Your school and conferences, I think, are the great cause of our people doing better here. . . . I know of fourteen persons that are saving and buying homes."[58] Another young leader wrote to Washington, "Our local conference is doing a good work and these people are taking hold with a will. . . . Our Conference is trying to buy 355 acres of land situated around the church. It will cost $1,775. Many individuals are also buying land and building houses."[59]

Earl Crosby published an article in 1977 discussing how Washington with his Tuskegee Conferences, with local conferences and agricultural extension programs and other means, such as Black agricultural fairs, helped southern rural Blacks to modernize and develop.[60] Du Bois especially, but also other Black writers, recorded the material progress that Blacks were making under oppressive conditions, praising the achievement but usually not mentioning that Washington, his young leaders, and his Tuskegee Machine were deeply involved in these successes. It was actually Du Bois and not Washington who came up with the name "Tuskegee Machine," which has always been used in retrospect. Washington did not have a name for the vast apparatus. Du Bois claimed that it was started to combat his northern Black opposition: "This beginning of organized opposition, together with other events, led to the growth at Tuskegee of what I have called the Tuskegee Machine."[61] This was Du Bois's way, in his *Autobiography*, of augmenting the image of Washington's opposition, showing that it was so formidable that Washington had to confront it with formidable means. The Machine had been initiated in 1881 when Washington began constructing Tuskegee Institute. By 1903–1905, it was a vast Machine that had the National Negro Business League as a part of it (Later the Urban League would be a part of it, which Washington helped to established). Louis Harlan had no idea when the Tuskegee Machine was established, and he thought that only Black people, and a limited group of them, were part of it. "Washington . . . built a powerful Tuskegee Machine among the black intellectuals, professional men, and businessmen in the Northern cities."[62] The Machine extended there and over such people, and also in southern cities, but this vast struture was centered in the South. It was a national structure, and it included powerful white people in it, which Harlan seemed not to have fathomed. Du Bois did. In his *Autobiography* he wrote, "Not only did presidents of the United States consult Booker T. Washington, but governors and congressmen; philanthropists conferred with him, scholars wrote to him. Tuskegee became a vast information bureau and center of advice."[63]

Looked at from the angle of modernization and development, Washington's Tuskegee Machine could be described as a "government." Blacks had no government that was interested in them or that they could significantly relate to, save Booker T. Washington and, through him, others. The Tuskegean created a "government" for Black people, stretched it across the length and width of Black America, but also into segments of the white population to attract people who could assist Blacks. He used this "government" to produce leaders, to implement programs, to try to modernize and develop Black America, and to try to draw the two segments of the Black community in America into a single one. The primary focus of the "government" was always Black people in the South, and Washington would not stand for northern Blacks (or Whites), living far away from the mass of Blacks, trying to lead them.

This was an early version of a contest that would emerge later in the twentieth century, when Third World countries would undergo modernization and development and the leaders of the process would have to deal with urban intellectuals and other educated or economic urban elements trying to be the main forces and leaders of the processes while significantly ignoring the rural people and their interests and desires, those who were in greatest need of modernization and development. It is interesting how some southern Whites were able to see what Washington was trying to do with Blacks in the South that his northern Black opposition were not able to see or did not want to see, and that many Black historians and other kinds of Black scholars and/or intellectuals have not seen because they have not studied the record. What some of these white southerners saw outraged them, and made them regard Washington as an enemy to Whites in the South. The rabid racist writer Thomas Dixon wrote the following:

Mr. Washington is not training Negroes to take their place in any industrial system in the South in which the white man can direct or control him. He is not training his students to be servants and come at the beck and call of any man. He is training them *all* to be masters of men, to be independent, to own and operate their own industries, plant their own fields, buy and sell their own goods, and in every shape and form destroy the last vestiage of dependence on the white man for anything.[64]

These were revolutionary objectives, by any definition. And most Black historians and other kinds of intellectuals remain ignorant of them, and a great deal else about Booker T. Washington that they should know about and that Black people today should know about. The time has come for Black historians to rethink the way they think about Washington. Historians who do not deal with evidence, or who are afraid to do so, or who do not feel it is necessary to do so, are individuals who have to rethink who they are and what they are doing. Booker T. Washington was the single most important person in Black history. It is time that Black historians became aware of that and conveyed this knowledge and understanding to Black people and other Americans.

Chapter 4

Black Women in Black and American History

In 1986 a symposium was published entitled *The State of Afro-American History*. It contained presented papers of a conference that had been held, involving Black and white historians, on where Black history stood in American history writing. There was a discussion of various themes in Black history and also of some related subjects. Black slavery, the Black urban experience, and the Black community were themes, accompanied by related topics such as Black history textbooks, teaching Black history in colleges and universities, and trends in Black history writing. There was commentary on the papers presented that appeared in the published book. There was an understanding that Black history should be integrated into the larger American history. Thomas Holt said the following about that in the introduction to the book:

Thus, Afro-American history becomes a window onto which the nation's history, a vantage point from which to reexamine and rewrite that larger history. This is true not simply because Blacks should be included for a more accurate portrait, but more because their inclusion changes many of the basic questions posed, the methods and sources for answering those questions, and the conclusions reached.[1]

Perhaps most people at the symposia did not know how old that point of view was. John Hope Franklin, who was at the conference and who delivered a paper "On the Evolution of Scholarship in Afro-American History," had stated that proposition thirty years before.[2] Thirteen years after that, Vincent Harding, who was also at the conference, expressed that view.[3] Four years after that, Benjamin Quarles proffered it.[4] Nathan Huggins, attending the conference as well, projected the view, and did so again at the meeting in his piece "Integrating Afro-American History into American History."[5] He noted how at one time most people thought "American history [was] the story of white men, and that [was] why blacks want[ed] a history of their own." He said the new social history had brought forth a strong interest in Black history and the plethora of writing on Black history, and also a landslide of writing on other neglected people in American history, which no longer made it possible to think of American history as simply white male history. But Huggins expressed his dissatisfaction with Black history just being included in American history. In the late 1970s he had said that it could be and was being included without significantly altering the main interpretation of American history: "The ethnic conception of American history persists," the white ethnic groups conception.[6] At the symposia, Huggins called for Black history to be used to provide a synthesis of American history:

We ought to see this work [Black history] as the building blocks of a new synthesis, a new American history. Would that the work should raise such fundamental questions of American society as to provoke discourse among American historians to change the history they write. We are able now to say, as we were not fifteen years ago, that blacks (black leaders, the black experience, etc.) are included in the textbooks.[7]

That was good, said Huggins, and it represented an advance in American history writing, but it was not good enough. There had to be a synthesis as a result of the inclusion of the material of Black history: "It cannot be told as a story of *black history* and *white history*. It must be told as one. While that idea is simple enough—a truism indeed—too few of us accept the radical implications of it. We do not put it into our thinking, our writing, our courses. That idea nevertheless, is a key to any new, successful narrative of American history."[8] In an article "Bias and Synthesis in History" that appeared in the *Journal of American History* years after the symposia, Nell Irvin Painter expressed her interest in an American history synthesis, which she said had to draw in Black men and women, white women, and other neglected groups such as "working people" as historical actors and agents. She argued that racism and these kinds of neglects had plagued efforts to write a meaningful synthesis of American history. The efforts of the 1950s, that had been glorified by the profession, had been in fact superficial efforts. They "claimed to encompass all the American people but spoke only of a small segment, white male elites, presenting an illusion of synthesis that was no synthesis at all."[9] Attempts at synthesis in later years had not advanced in a substantial way because of the continuing plague of racist and other encumbrances that led to the exclusion of people or a diminishment of their presence in a work of synthesis.

If one takes Painter's writing and links it to that of John Hope Franklin's piece in 1957, one is talking about Black historians over a period of forty years calling for Black history to be a basis for writing an American history synthesis. The repeated references to it indicate clearly that it has not been done, and would also seem to indicate that Black historians have no interest in doing so. The only area of American history where Black historians show any significant interest in syntehsis is the period of the mid-nineteenth-century war and the reconstruction efforts that followed it. Nell Painter wrote a text on the late nineteenth and early twentieth centuries entitled *Standing at Armageddon*. If this was her effort at writing an American history synthesis, it was not a significant accomplishment in that genre. There were large stretches of writing and even whole chapters where Black people were not mentioned. Where they were mentioned it usually amounted to a simple integration, with no effort to pose new questions or to reinterpret this period of American history or episodes or actions in it. The chapter "Race and Disfranchisement" was written essentially apart from the larger American history. The material itself should have posed the question of whether America was a democratic society, and also raised questions about the differences between representative government and democratic government. The best that Painter would say was that the racist disfranchisement of Blacks "circumscribed democracy," with the implication that America was a democratic society even when it practiced political exclusion or political suppression.[10]

And what she had to say about Blacks and their actions was not a basis for writing in a very critical manner about the "Progressive Era," which she did in a separate chapter. Blacks were mentioned twice. The "Progressive Era" was not based on the assumption of its white supremacist/ebonicistic, or its maleist/sexist foundations, which would raise or should have raised questions about calling this period of American history the "Progressive Era." It was at a minimum the "Progressive/-Oppressive Era," which would beg for new descriptions and images. Incredibly, no connection was made between the oppression/suppression of Blacks in the South, the consequential power for southern white men in the U.S. government, and the inability of the American Socialist Party to become a major political party in the country. Nor was the very strong racism of America's white socialists that Du Bois and other Black socialists complained about drawn in as a reason for the party's inability. When talking about the socialists, Painter preferred to use the term "social class," and did not talk about racism or race.

One thing is for sure: Black historians will not take up the task of writing an American history synthesis, or even show an interest in considering it, let alone doing it, until they start thinking larger than Black history. There is a very narrow focus on that subject by Black historians, as if Black history takes place in a vacuum in America, as if it is not related significantly to America. There is no great interest on the part of Black historians to write on white people except in a fleeting and necessary manner. And they have to be ready to face criticisms that will come from many Black historians if they endeavor to do so. Black women historian Darlene Clark Hine experienced that dissent and cricitism, as did Nell Painter and Wilma King. Hine experienced distressing comments when she wrote an introduction to the new edition of Katharine Du Pre Lumpkin's autobiography, *The Making of a Southerner*.[11]

There are not many Black women historians in America, and Black women's history is considerably still under-researched and under-written. It is a new field in American history writing, and it has some seeds to sow. But this argument about the lack of Black women historians is not as commanding as it might appear. There are many Black historians in America now, and the overwhelming number of them have Ph.Ds. But one does not find any significant writing on American history coming from these historians, save for the war and reconstruction period. No texts (save for Painter's), no monographs, not even any efforts to write something of a limited nature on Black and white people in America, in a period of American history, or in an American historical episode or situation. A larger number of Black women historians, as this experience shows, will not lead to them either writing on anything much other than Black women, and it will mainly be Black women within Black hsitory and not within American history.

But there are Black women historians, like Black male historians, who have called for Black history to be a basis for reinterpreting the larger American history. There has even been a call to employ Black women's history as a basis for reinterpreting American history. Darlene Clark Hine has that interest. She has stated that all the writing she had done on Black women's history had been done not just to throw extensive light on that subject but to establish the basis for "centering Black women in American history." Looking at that larger history from that perspective can be done, and could produce some startling revelations about America and startling observations about the role that Black women have played in American history and their contributions to it. I intend to speak to that matter later in this chapter.

The "centering" of Black women's history in the larger American history would require what it would also take to "center" it in Black history: a very accurate view of Black women's history. That is in the making, in the hands of Black women historians and also from contributions from white women historians writing on the subject. But there has to be an understanding that "centering" Black women in either of these broader histories is the centering of a limited subject matter and perspective. Black women have criticized and continue to criticize Black male historians for writing Black history as if all Black people were men, and as if only Black men have made Black history. There are Black male historians who express concern that Black women historians will simply try to put the shoe on the other foot and diminish the historical role and contributions of Black men to Black history. Some also express concern about the effects this will have on Black male–female relations, the functioning of the Black community, and even Black political strength in the country. Nell Painter was a commentator at the symposia and she spoke to these concerns and potential serious troublespots:

The indisposition to see black women's history as a legitimate field is weakening considerably, and today black women's history is seldom seen as undermining black unity. Yet some recent writing includes passages that seem to pit black women against black men in a contest for the claim of the most oppressed. Even now, concentration on the history of black women is sometimes seen as a veiled attack on black men, or on "the black man."[12]

Painter feels there is an overreaction involved here, because Black men and women are different and have had different experiences in Black history, and each should be able to reveal this experience; indeed, it is imperative to make disclosures, and it is something that Black women historians have to do because Black women's history is only now coming into focus and development and there is much more work to do on the subject. Of course, Black women's history is not isolated from Black men and the way they have made history within Black history. Obviously Black men and Black women have impacted each other. The ways this has happened is something that Black women historians and Black women's history could throw much light on, because they are oriented to understanding how Black women have fared in Black history, and that has always been related to their intereaction with Black men, but also with white men and white women. It seems that there is going to be a lengthy period of time in the writing of Black history and Black women's history. There will come a time when Black history will have to be fully integrated and synthesized, which will produce what could be called *Black Ourstory* (that would be expanded to *Black American Ourstory*).

It is an interesting thing in the writing of Black women's history that Black women historians did not show any initial interest in writing it. They had been convinced, it would seem, by Black men, and white men and women, that Black women's history was not a valid or viable subject, nor should it be or could it be. This was also the history of racism, white supremacy/ebonicism, and sexism, and the history of Black people in America working on the thinking of these historians, even Ph.D. professional ones, to disregard Black women's history. Darlene Clark Hine, who has become one of the most important Black women historians in America, could remember how she had a negative view toward Black women's history and regarded writing on it as a distinct waste of time. She was finally convinced by a woman in Indiana, Shirley Herd, against her own resistance to the latter's importuning to write on the history of Black women in Indiana. As she looked back on her coming of age as a Black woman historian, Hine remarked in her book *Hine Sight*, "When I decided to become a historian the last group I intended to study was Black women. During the 1960s, Black history included race but not gender."[13] Hine viewed her book of 1979, *Black Victory: The Rise and Fall of the White Primary in Texas*, to be a book about race. It was not until five years later that she even became aware of the subject of Black women's history. Shirley Herd, a school teacher in an Indiana town and president of the National Council of Negro Women, put it on her mind. At the time the importuning began she was a Ph.D. teaching in Indiana and was silent about Black women in Black and American history. Shirley Herd noticed that. In 1981 Hine published a history of Black women in Indiana, *When the Truth is Told*, and also vowed that she would never neglect or minimize Black women's history again: "I will never again write a history that excludes or marginalizes Black women or fails to consider their work as makers of community."[14]

Hine appeared at the symposia in 1986 and presented a paper titled, "Lifting the Veil, Shattering the Silence: Black Women's

History in Slavery and Freedom," in which she made a plea to the historians at the conference, and Black historians and white historians generally writing in Black history, not to forget or neglect the history of Black women in Black and American history. In *Hine Sight*, which was published eight years later, Hine spoke with general approval of the accomplishments of Black women's historiography:

We now know that black women have played essential roles in ensuring the survival of black people under slavery and of black communities in freedom. . . .

Through the myriad voluntary associations and club activities in the late nineteenth and twentieth centuries, black women created and sustained innumerable churches, hospitals, schools, clinics, day-care centers, neighborhood improvement projects, and protest organizations. Black women working in tandem with black men founded migration clubs and relocated themselves and their families in western towns and northern cities. And throughout these survival struggles they played instrumental roles—although too often unheralded—in laying the groundwork for the modern civil rights revolution.[15]

But notwithstanding what she felt Black women had achieved in Black history and helping to make that history, Hine felt there was still something missing in the writing of Black women's history, something that made her feel "disquieted." She explained what it was:

Too little attention has been devoted to the working-class status of black women. The fact is that the vast majority of black women have lived in overwhelming poverty, and a lack of attention to that fact has helped to foster erroneous impresions in the larger society of the mythical, heroic, transcendent black woman able to do the impossible, to make a way out of no way.[16]

Another source of disquiet for Hine is her view that there is not enough attention paid to the "intersection" of historical or social factors in the writing of Black women's history. In any intersectional analysis, she asserted, social class has to be included: "If we truly intend to do intersectional analyses then class must occupy as much attention as race and sex."[17] She also referred to the intersection of race and class. There are other Black women historians who take this view. Nell Painter is one:

In large part, I suspect that the reluctance with which many of us juggle variables in addition to race is rooted in the conviction, not always mistaken, that the addition of class, gender, or regional considerations to race is less an honest attempt to write history more sensitively than a subterfuge, a way of downplaying racial oppression and mitigating its severity. Adding other considerations to race is often interpreted as saying that racial oppression was not really very bad. Although the skepticism may make sense politically, it stifles the careful analysis of what Afro-Americans did and thought in the past.[18]

What is missing from the intersectional analysis of Hine, Painter, and other Black women historians, and from the intersectional analysis of Black female feminists (or Black womanists, as some Black women call themselves) is *racism*. In America, that phenomenon would be the nexus of any "cross-racial" intersectional analysis. Many Black women historians and feminists or womanists do not really know what racism is, nor the distinction between race and racism. bell hooks has focused attention on the concept of racism in her writing, but she shows only a slight understanding of what it means, because invariably she juxtaposes it to sexism, as she did in *Ain't I a Woman*, where she remarked, "Consequently, when the women's movement raised the issue of sexist oppression, we argued that sexism was insignificant in the light of the harsher, more brutal reality of racism. We were afraid to acknowledge that sexism could be just as oppressive as racism."[19] In her book *Yearning* she concentrated analytical attention on the intersection of sexism and gender, without realizing that sexism was a form of racism, and that it was racism that impacted Black and white female gender.[20] On the other hand, she intersected racism with race, not extensively, but always viewing racism as associated exclusively with race. And Black and white feminists like to use the word *Other*. White and Black male writers and others do the same, and they use it with racism to the extent that they deal with that term, and always as if it is associated only with race. As said in a previous chapter, racist beliefs produce "Non-Others," not Others, a "race" or "races" that are outside of humanity, that are "races" of "gods" or "godlike" "entities," and "races" of "nonhumans" or "subhumans." Other is or should be a reference to actuality, to actual existing human forms, such as race, gender, ethnic group, social class, or regional group, all of which can have racist beliefs devised for them to make "races" of them and then endeavor to impose the "races" on these actualities. "Non-Others" is not a concept for the mass of historians of any kind, or for the mass of social writers in America today. But when they use the concept Other, they are really talking about "Non-Others" without knowing it, just as people in Western history for centuries have talked about race, meaning "race" and not understanding that or knowing it.

Black feminist theorist Patricia Hill Collins has taken great pride in the way Black women have broken through the cultural silence that has been imposed on them in American history and society by white men, white women, and Black men. Of course, the silence was never complete, as it never could be. As Collins said, Black women always talked about their oppressed situation to each other. And then there was the breaking of silence that Black women did throughout their history and the history of Black people in this country when they engaged in actions in the Black social world that were verbal and practical, to help make Black history and to help build the Black ethnic group and the Black ethnic community. The continued and multiple ways that Black women have always broken through the imposed silence in America has to act as a restraint on making blanket remarks about this silence. The silence that has been broken, which Collins knows well enough, is the breaking through of the societal public silence that has been imposed on Black women in a very strong manner thorughout their history in this country. American society has never heard or known of a Black Woman's Voice. But that Voice has surfaced and is becoming powerful, and it is, as Frederick Douglass said, "rattling the air." Collins made these remarks about Black women breaking through the societal public silence:

Much of the public voice that Black women gained in the 1980s represents a dare. Because individual African-American women broke silence in multiple arenas. Black women's collective voice is now public and known. Such voice challenges the legitimacy of public transcripts claiming Black female inferiority. Because it represents profound public insubordination, this newly public voice was bound to generate new forms of suppression dedicated to resilencing African-American women.[21]

One of those sources of suppression or a source to attempt suppression will be white women, including white female feminists. It would be an effort most likely made by white female feminists, who have already impacted Black women historians and Black feminist or Black womanist thinkers. White female feminist thinkers generally no longer employ the word or concept sexism, and prefer to use concepts like gender and patriarchy or patriarchical, and, of course, social class. Only a few ever knew that sexism was a form of racism, as Marlene Dixon knew and proclaimed in the early 1970s: "The very stereotypes that express the society's belief in the biological inferiority of women recall the images to justify the oppression of Blacks." She then went on to say, equally perceptively, "The fact that 'racism' has been practiced against many groups other than Blacks has been pushed into the background."[22] This was shades of Du Bois, profound and insightful, and like Du Bois's understanding on this matter, not understood, ignored, and/or pushed from thought and consciousness and public writings. White female feminists discovered that they did not like Black feminists using the concept of sexism and associating it with their condition. The constant reference to it brought white feminists, and in their minds, white women, too close to the conception and condition of Black women; that Black and white women were in the same boat in America.

White female feminists did not want that perception to be a strong public one. They felt their own distance from Black female feminists, and especially the Black womanists, who emphasized Blackness or blackness in writing about Black women and their issues or struggles, and felt leagues apart from the mass of Black women. Concepts like gender, social class, and patriarchy came to the rescue, primarily the rescue of having to deal with the most dreaded subject of all for white female feminists, as it is for white male thinkers of all kinds: racism; namely, white supremacy/ebonicism. They fear being called racists, or having their racism exposed. The shadow of Nazism edges up, and the fear of being called racist or having their racism exposed, because they either know or have some suspicion of how they identify with or cling to that reality.

White female feminists, like other white women in America, see themselves as part of the *white majority* of the country, and very comfortably use the concepts "minority," "racial minority," "racial minorities," "black" or "Black minority," and "ethnic minority," meaning only the ethnic groups of dark hue in America. Minority is a word that connotes marginalization, not belonging, or not belonging fully, of being less important, less deserving, or making less of an impact. Too many white female feminists come out of this bag, this racist thinking bag. It is not something they will admit, and will usually fiercely deny. But sometimes the reality has been admitted, as was done by Barbara Hilkert Andolsen:

Racism is a social reality that can best be seen not by focusing on the overt intentions of whites, but on the unfair advantage accruing to whites at the expense of blacks. All white women, including white feminists, have privileged positions as *white persons* in American society. All white women, including white feminists, participate in institutions that sustain that racial privilege. "All of us are born into an environment where racism exists. Racism affects all of our lives, but it is only white women who can 'afford' to remain oblivious to those effects."[23]

White women, like white men, are overwhelmingly born into a White social world in America. White supremacy/ebonicism still heavily inundates this world, as well as other forms of racism, including maleism/sexism. The racism, in any form, is not strictly deterministic in this world, in the culture and institutions, or intellectually or psychologically. Whites vary in their imbibement of racism or racisms, and in the afflictions of these perverse phenomena. Some even manage to escape the interpenetrations of racism, which is too complicated to go into here. Historically, white men have been and continue to be the main intellectuals and the main public voice of the White social world. They have likewise been the main intellectuals and the main voice of Western history and civilization, and in America the main intellectuals and voice in American history, culture, and society. White female feminists in America have been able to fully break through the public silence that white men have historically imposed upon them, and have established the White Woman's Voice, which white female feminists immediately projected as the *universal* woman's voice in Western civilization and in America. There is also the idea that the white woman's social experience in Western civilization and America was the universal woman's social experience, the legacy of the European Enlightenment and, even more accurately, its continuation through white feminist thinking and writing.

Most of these women would see themselves as postmodern thinkers attacking the Englightenment metaphysical philosophical foundational thinking, like the white male postmodern thinkers claim they are doing. But all the latter really did was to emphasize aspects of thought that Enlightenment thinkers would not have done, such as relativism instead of universalism, or difference instead of similarity or plurality rather than unity or consensus, or local rather than universal or absolute. The white male postmodern thinkers were clever or astute enough to avoid trying to ground their brand of thinking in deep, foundational philosophical soil. But since they would not give any credence to the intellectual or philosophical categories of the Englightenment, and regard their own beliefs and analytical categories as the only ones having credence and validity, they, in effect, made their beliefs and analytical categories a priori foundational structures.

White female feminist thinkers and writers were not as clever as their white male counterparts, because they came out projecting universalist thought about women, women's history, and women's social experience. They did this because they took this kind of thinking from white men. And they also took from them the practice of grounding historical, cultural, or social thought in racist premises or *racist foundationalism*. And like their white male mentors, they did not know they were doing this or did not understand that they were, or how much, and like them are ready immediately to deny that this was what they were doing or what they intended doing. It was an "unconscious" thing at best, they might say, which was another way of them saying that the racism was embedded in them—beyond their awareness or understanding—and that unconscious thinking itself was just a different form of intentional thinking.

Black women feminists reacted to the universalist thinking and writing by white female feminists, seeing the racism and making the charge but also ranking behind the very notion that the experience of Black women in America was the same as the experience of white women. Alternative Black feminist thinking was born, and through the agency of Alice Walker, the Black womanist concept. The late poet Audre Lorde once remarked, "The master's tools will never dismantle the master's house. They may enable us temporarily to beat him at his own game, but they will never enable us to bring about genuine change."[24] Lorde was fully aware of the racism of white female feminists and the feminist movement, which was mainly a movement of middle-class white women. She had her intellectual battles with the white feminist religious thinker Mary Daly. But what seems necessary for Black women historians and other Black female intellectuals is to modify Lorde's insight by extending it to white female thinkers and other white women. Actually, this has been done, but not from this prompting, as Black feminist alternative feminist thinking and Black womanism exist. But the need of this kind of behavior is not as conscious and diligent as it should be, because Black women historians and Black feminist or Black womanists are continuing to take categories of thinking and concepts from white feminist thinkers (or from white male postmodern thinkers) without being cautious enough about that or critical enough in employing them, and not using Black history to test their validity, especially with respect to analyzing the history and social life of Blacks in the country.

As seen, Darlene Clark Hine, Nell Painter, and others, such as Angela Davis, bell hooks, and Evelyn Brooks Higginbotham, would like to see Black women historians or Black woman analysts use the concept and analytical device of social class in their writings. But the use so far, as far as I have been able to determine by looking at these various sources, is that social class is used as inadequately and erroneously as white historians and other kinds of white analysts use it. There is, after all, no such thing as a "working class" or an "underclass." History has shown and continues to show that all social classes work, in the home or outside the home. And history continues to show that all classes below the upper class in a society or community are "underclasses." Ideology or concepts have replaced history and sociology or sociological analysis. This is the legacy of Karl Marx and the Marxists or other kinds of socialists that appeared in Western history and civilization, who were able to spread their ideas, concepts, and methods of historical and social analysis to the far reaches of the world.

Historians, political scientists, politicians, philosophers, and a host of others have tried to determine what Karl Marx meant by social class. They have all continued to miss the point that he continued to make about it: that a social class was men, or the male gender. Marx was like the bourgeois intellectuals before him, intellectuals of the Enlightenment like himself, who equated social class with men. Women were *invisibilized*, because the bourgeois analysts, Marx, the Marxists, and others spoke and wrote about social class on the basis of a maleist/sexist premise or racist foundationalism. Karl Marx and the Marxists even went so far as to make economic or professional occupational groups social classes, which is why people interpreted his concept to mean economic class. Marx never had a social-class concept or analysis, in fact. He always employed a group analysis, or a subdivision of that analysis, when he analyzed economic or professional groups, who for him were always comprised of men. When Marx said capitalist, he meant a male, even if he never made a reference to gender. In America, capitalist was always understood to mean white male, even though race and gender were not part of the description or the narrative or analytical discussion. It was Black people who had to impress upon white people that Black people could be capitalists. Booker T. Washington promoted that idea in a very strong manner, saying that both Black men and Black women could become capitalists. His National Negro Business League was made up of Black men and women.

Black people could not be said to have had social classes throughout much of their history. On that basis alone, there would have to be a cautious use of that concept, and likely some different kind of conceptualization would have to be devised. There have always been Black people in Black history, male and female, who had power and prestige among Blacks that could not be attributed to any class factors. Some of the household slaves, male and female, had prestige and standing with other slaves because they could overhear conversations and pass information along. A Black man who worked in the home of wealthy white people, or who was their carriage driver or later their chauffeur, might have prestige and standing among Blacks in their own community. More than one Black janitor or Pullman Porter or numbers player had prestige and significant power or influence in the Black community. Mother Clara Hale had great prestige among Blacks in Harlem for years because of the good things she did for Black children. The significance that Harriet Tubman, Sojourner Truth, Margaret Washington (Booker

T. Washington's wife), Rosa Parks, Coretta Scott King, Fannie Lou Hamer, or Ella Baker had among Blacks in their communities in the South or throughout the region was not based on their class status or any of the criteria that could be employed to determine that. They had status, power, and prestige because of what they did to help Black people.

Booker T. Washington epitomized this criteria for determining power, influence, and status among Blacks, and Du Bois also demonstrated this primary criteria. Black sociologist William Julius Wilson alerted Black people to the fact that social classes were developing in a full way, or at least a fuller manner among them, in his book *The Declining Significance of Race*, and it was this book and other of Wilson's writings on Black social class that have had an impact on Black historians and other kinds of intellectuals.[25] But a class analysis as a general concept and analytical device has to include, at a minimum, men and women, since they are both of the class, and also, at a minimum, the cultural orientation of that class. Neither the male, the female, or the culture of the class can be made synonymous with the class as if no one or nothing else existed and everything had been said. But even with this understanding of social class, and even if it were worked out to an effective degree as a concept and analytical tool, these devices would still be problematic conceptually and in efforts to use them to analyze Black history or Black women's history, where nonclass factors have always had and still have strong determinant qualities; particularly, deeds done.

Today, white female feminist writers make great use of the words or concepts of patriarch, patriarchy, or patriarchichal. Many Black women historians, feminist writers, or womanist writers have assimilated these constructs and used them in their spoken and written efforts, as their white feminist counterparts make use of them. There have been some Black male supporters of Black women writers' use of these concepts. One of them has been the Black literary critic Michael Awkward, who regards Black feminist or womanist thought, or Black male supportive feminist thought, as all being antipatriarchical and thought that assists Black women in carving out and holding a space for their own subjectivity in Black history and social life. Awkward even sees these three intellectual efforts against Black male patriarchy making space for Black men and Black women to form bonds or unity between themselves to strengthen Black life in America. He in fact insists upon "the joint participation of black males and females as *comrades*."[26] Black women historians are employing the concepts of patriarch or patriarchal in their writings as a way of speaking about the Black male historical domination or suppression of Black women, to be able to disclose that fact and also to widen the perception and understanding of the role that Black women have played in Black history, which can no longer be denied.

But it has to be said that Black women historians and other kinds of Black female thinkers, and also supportive Black male thinkers, such as Lewis Gordon or Devon Carbado, employ the concept of patriarchy inadequately. Devon Carbado wrote,

[To] the extent that black men ignore the particularities of black women's racial experiences or exclude themselves from discussions about gender dynamics in the black community, they are unlikely to come to terms with . . . the patriarchal privilege they wield. Nor are they likely to challenge the notion that black men, and not black women, represent the paradigm of Black being.[27]

This observation carries an appearance of truth, as do the Black women historian and Black female feminist and Black womanist uses of the concepts of patriarch or patriarchal in their spoken or written efforts. But it is nothing more than an appearance and not an actuality of patriarchy or patriarchical domination in Black history. There has been very little Black male patriarchy in Black history. This word continues to be used in an inappropriate fashion by Black and white female thinkers, and a whole host of other thinkers, whether it is historicized, as Marxist female feminists employ it, or whether it is contextualized, which is the typical female or male feminist usage. The word patriarchy has been used like the word sexism, not knowing or not accepting what it really meant. Concepts are not just ideational things that are constructed abstractly. They come out of the historical process and relate to that process. It is history that plays a very prominent role in determining the authenticity and legitimacy of concepts. They might just be fanciful constructions, as racism amply demonstrates, with no reference to reality or any kind of embodiment. History indicates when a concept changes into another concept, and indicates when a concept is being used that no longer relates to the reality it was originally associated with, because that reality no longer exists or no longer has noticeable embodiment. And history shows where different concepts that mean different things are used interchangeably as if they meant the same thing. Liberalism and democracy are two different words denoting two different political realities, but in America they are commonly used, by intellectuals of many kinds, to say nothing about politicians, as if they meant the same thing. It is like the confused understanding about race and racism, and the way they are commonly used interchangeably. The words sexuality and gender are used interchangeably. Sex is even equated with gender, which is what Darlene Clark Hine did in the following remark, already alluded to: "If we truly intend to do intersectional analyses then class must occupy as much attention as race and sex."

Intersectional analysis requires *concept integrity*, and that cannot be determined simply abstractly or analytically, as analytical philosophers might do; and certainly not simply ideologically. History also has to be employed to determine how the concept has been used over time. Gender is a concept like ethnic group. In each case, there is a biological, cultural, and social dimension, even a historical dimension. Sexuality has to do with biology, and sex has to do with a limited physical act. Sexuality can include a large number of things, or a large number of things can be associated with it to help define it: bodily parts, bodily movements (especially walking, hip, or shoulder movements), certain gestures, clothes, cosmetics, and other things short of the sexual act itself. Black psychiatrist Gail Elizabeth Wyatt has described the historical abuse of the sexuality of Black women:

But the depersonalization of black women focuses on our sexuality first. In our homes, in our neighborhoods and around the world, powerful stereotypes rooted in slavery perpetuate myths about who we are. Society's message is that to be black and female is to be without sexual control, to be irresponsible about our sexuality. Regardless of the circumstances, our age or our appearance, someone may assume that we are sexually available or for sale at some price.[28]

The abuse of Black women's sexuality, historically, as Wyatt was indicating, was to reduce it down to the sex act and Black women being licentious in regard to that, or even gearing their own sexuality to that limited activity, encouraging others to notice what they were doing. So when Black women historians or Black feminist or womanist writers say that Black men have dominated Black women's sexuality, or phrase it as the Black man's sexual domination of women, what does that mean? This would not mean, or should not mean, the domination of Black women with respect to the sex act. And it does not and should not mean Black male gender domination of the Black female gender. These are all separate things and cannot all mean the same thing in depicting them in the writing of Black women's history, or Black feminist or womanist thought. It does not disclose historical or social truth, and instead projects fantasies, distortions, and untruths.

This also and clearly applies to the Black women's use of patriarch, patriarchy, or patriarchal, or their use by their Black male supporters. Human history shows that the notion, practice, or word patriarchy referred fundamentally to men dominating men. This was always the great problem of domination. Long before many of the institutions appeared in human history to make that possible, there was always age, experience, wisdom, and longevity of memory that could be employed, and whose employment would also be encouraged as they were ways to reduce violence in a group's political and social life. The oldest male could become the ultimate group authority, and he would be the patriarch. There could be a number of such individuals, who would then be classified as patriarchs, and might even form a council, which might be dubbed a "council of elders," which history shows has usually been a council of men. Tribes or villages had patriarchs, as did extended families. Dominating men assured the domination of women and children.

In single families or extended families, fathers sought to dominate their male children or their sons. These were the individuals who had to preserve the family name, which women would not do, marrying outside the family. The son or sons would be the principle heirs of property or wealth, even if it were inherited through a matrilineal line of descent. In ancient Kemet (Egypt), pharaohship was legitimized through matrilineal descent, but only a male could legally occupy the throne. Patriarchy produced male subordination to men, but also unity among men against women. The patriarch of a family dominated women, and patriarchs of tribes, clans, or villages dominated women, and did so through other men. But these men also dominated the children, boys and girls, which means that patriarchy was also related to the domination of families by men, and this was basic domination and a basic meaning of the concept. Patriarchy was not related specifically to male–female relations, or specifically to male domination of women. These things were predicated on something else: maleism/sexism.

Maleism/sexism said to men that they were a "race" of "gods" or "godlike" "entities," and that women were a "race" of "nonhumans" or "subhumans," which could also be related to creature or animal, or thing, or property. When applied to human beings, this rejects their humanity and is predicated on and reflects racist beliefs. Creatures, animals, property, or objects are all things that can be owned. What maleism/sexism said to men was that they had a right to own women, and on that basis they could dominate them, just as they did anything else that they owned. Du Bois saw this matter with great clarity. In 1922, in *The Crisis*, he wrote, "We have always realized, the . . . question is at bottom simply a matter of ownership of women."[29] Unfortunately, this is not something that has ever been realized widely, and today in America and elsewhere it is being obscured from view and understanding. In America, feminist thinkers of all kinds are doing so. White female feminists took the lead in doing this, because they were looking for concepts and words to keep from having to deal with racism. They also did not want to think of their experience in America as being the same as that of Black women, who had a history of being slaves and being owned, and even owned by white women, which was also something to avoid contemplating or dealing with as often as possible because the reality of female ownership would be perceived and understood. Male domination of women seemed better to white female feminists than male ownership of women, so they latched onto the concept of patriarchy and bent it to their needs. And they passed it on to Black women historians and other Black female and male thinkers in a mangled manner, where it ends up in distorted use in their speeches or written work.

bell hooks wrote, for instance, in *Yearning*, "Insistence on patriarchical values, on equating black liberation with black men gaining access to male privilege that would enable them to assert power over black women, was one of the most significant forces undermining radical struggle."[30] bell hooks's central value is *radicalism*, because of her socialist orientation, as it is for Manning Marable. And for both of them it significantly suppresses any other kind of perception or fact about Black history. In hooks's case it suppresses her ability to deal conceptually and analytically with patriarchy, which is a term she uses uncritically. This is just like Michele Wallace, who had earlier made a similar remark about Black men in the Black struggle for full freedom in America in *Black Macho*.[31] The overwhelming reason that Black men assumed or attempted to assume ascendancy in this great struggle is because they knew, as white men knew, that the latter would never give the struggle a thought if it were led by Black women. They reacted extremely negatively to white women carrying out their own struggle, negatively toward their own wives, daughters, sisters, or nieces. Their reaction to Black women would have been even more extreme, and their reaction to Black men, whom they perceived not to be leaders, and being led by women, would have been one of ridicule and great loathing, if not pure hatred, which would likely have resulted in extensive violence against Black men accompanied by a persistent mocking of them for having to be "protected" by their women.

Patriarchical beliefs or values have never been strong among Black men or significant sources of motivation for their behavior against Black women, and still less against white women. To believe this and to say or write this is simply to ignore centuries of white people functioning as racists, and especially strongly as white supremacists/ebonicists in American history, and the deep and extensive way they invested their racism in that history and in American culture and social life that mobilized American history, culture, and society against Black people. For Black men and Black women, the overriding task they both had was protecting themselves, their children, and their families from the great White racist menace that was all around them every day of their existence, and that could come in on them, and often did in a very vicious manner. This great need to protect self, children, and family was not motivated by patriarchical beliefs or values; if so, then these beliefs and values would also have to have been those of Black women as well, because they also had the same enemy and the same thing to protect themselves from. What has always been a matter of great concern to Black men in their history was not patriarchy, domination, or control of anybody, but how, simply, to be *men* in a country that denied their manhood. Black women were under that same kind of gun, and had an overriding task of trying to be women and demonstrating their womanhood. Both groups of Blacks had white models in front of them, and both groups, by observation, hearsay, or from their own experience, knew that they could get cut down, in a number of ways, for trying to emulate the models publicly. They could also receive flack from some Blacks within the Black social world, who would accuse them of being white, or trying to be white.

But what the focus on patriarchy among Black men in Black history or Black social life also does, as something detrimental to the writing on and understanding of these things, is to suppress the real meaning of patriarchy, and also the reason why white feminists thinkers took up with it, and also the real thing that motivated the male's relationship to a woman: ownership. The meaning of patriarchy is men dominating men and all members of a family, which could not have applied to many Black men in America, because for centuries most Black men were slaves and were not permitted to dominate other men or to dominate Black women or children. These two groups and Black men were owned by white men or white women, and these people dominated them precisely because they owned them. After Black chattel slavery was abolished in the 1860s, there was a time of nonslavery for Blacks in America. But in the 1880s, and even before, many Blacks started slipping into a new form of servitude associated with generational sharecropping, generational indebtedness, peonage, policed plantations, county sheriff repression, political disfranchisement, and violence. This new form of servitude went on into the 1940s, when it began breaking up. The new servitude had many of the same kinds of restrictions on Black men and Black women, in regard to Black manhood and Black womanhood, as the older form. Most Blacks lived in the South, and those who were not in the new bondage—and millions were (and this was one of Washington's and his youthful Black leaders greatest struggles, trying to keep Blacks from falling into it, or trying to get them out of it, which Washington called the "mortgage system")—were subjected to the racist whims and racist violence of white men, which could include just simply coming into a Black man's house to do violence, or doing it to a Black man, woman, or child in their front or back yard. A Black man, especially, perceived to be "uppity," could find the Ku Klux Klan, or some other white terrorist group coming after him or his family.

As said, Black women historians and other Black women writers or Black male writers have to be careful in the borrowing of concepts for conceptual or analytical purposes. Borrowed concepts are concepts that someone else has devised for their own purposes. They might not be applicable to another people or another situation. Oppressed people, struggling people, have to devise their own concepts and definitions, based on a solid evaluation and understanding of their own history and social life, which will be analytical devices. One can readily see the absurdity of trying to apply a concept of ownership to the relationship between Black men and Black women (although there were some Black male slaveholders who owned some Black men, women, and children). In addition, between the two, Black women had the greater independence in Black life; they were the ones who could find work when Black men could not, the ones who could get out of the Black world more easily, and the ones who might even assimilate American culture more than Black men, even if the latter had greater access to education. Many of the things that Black women did to help build the Black community, in time and over time in America, were things they saw white women do, or participated in with white women, as cooks, maids, servants of various kinds, or even as live-in companions. But these were also things that Black women could observe and learn from a distance.

Equally of limited value to Black women historians, or Black feminists or womanists, and distortive of their verbal or written efforts, is the inadequate way they use intersectional analysis, which they do by considerably imitating their white female counterparts. As seen, race and class have been distorted and used erroneously by all these groups. Gender has been used interchangeably with sex, sexism has not been understood as racism, sexuality has been equated with gender. And all of these groups do not want to deal with racism at all or very much. As said before, there has to be concept integrity for effective and meaningful intersectional analysis. To deal with American history, culture, and social life, one has to put racism—namely, white supremacy/ebonicism—at the nodal point of any intersectional analysis between white people and Black people and any intersectional regional or societal analyses. One gets the impression that a major reason why Black women historians or feminist or womanist thinkers don't use a racist analysis is because they are afraid of offending white female feminists or other white women, knowing how they fear the subject, do not want to hear it, and invariably seek to avoid it, consciously or unconsciously. If this is a strong motivation then one has to ask if this is accommodating white women, or "accommodationism," and which one of these Black women would be on firm ground to label Booker T. Washington an "accommodationist" in the sense of it being pejorative, and as something they themselves do not do? When the radical bell hooks, or Patricia Collins, or Joy James speak of race or the race factor, do not understand that sexism is a form of racism, and emphasize class and gender, they are avoiding racism, or greatly minimizing it in their analyses or theories, and therefore are "accommodating" white female feminists and white women, and feeding their delusions about who they are and what they are doing in America. What they are mainly doing is struggling against white men and trying to achieve things against them and working out things with them in America to have a greater share in dominating and running the country. White women have never seen themselves struggling in this country against Black men, Indian men, Hispanic men, or Asian men. Only white men. For years they struggled on their own, and did not want Black women involved in *their* struggle, which led Sojourner Truth to ask the question, both personally and generically, "Ain't I a Woman?" Shirley J. Yee documents how white female abolitionists did not want Black women in their groups, and did not want to work with Black women to end Black slavery.[32] And white suffragettes had "No Negroes Allowed" or "No Colored Allowed" signs over their efforts. It was the Black Liberation Movement of the 1950s and 1960s that led to the resurrection and intensity of the white feminist movement, and that brought benefits to it and white women. Their ingratitude would have been luminous if it had not been acknowledged, and that acknowledgment and benefit seemed logically to call for Black and white women getting together or becoming political allies. But then white female feminists began to talk in their racist predicate universalist terms to keep distance between themselves and other white women and Black women. In American history, or in Black history, White racism (i.e., white supremacy/ebonicism) and an ability to develop and use that form of analysis is the critical analytical device that out-weighs all the others, which are not equal to it, although a racist analysis must be used in conjunction with other conceptual analy-ses that will function to establish the limits of the other analyses and the racist analysis itself.

I want to conclude this chapter by coming back to an idea ad-vanced by Darlene Clark Hine, her interest in "centering Black women in American history." This seems to me an important and necessary investigative and analytical action in which Black women historians should engage. Years ago Black journalist and historian Paula Giddens wrote a popular book on Black women's history called *When and Where I Enter*.[33] The title came from Julia Anna Cooper, a Black intellectual of the late nineteenth and early twentieth cen-turies, who raised the question about how Black women fitted into American life. They entered American life early and fitted into it early and in a rather peculiar but awesome manner.

First black African women and then Black women entered Ameri-can history as slaves during the colonial prenational phase of that history. In the first half of the nineteenth century white men would be debating each other publicly, and sometimes white women, with respect to the place of white women in the new American national-ity or national identity and in American life.[34] No debate went on about where Black women fitted in. That matter had been settled back in the 1660s. That was when laws were passed that estab-lished Black slavery, or de facto practices did, which explicitly or interpretatively barred others from being slaves in America, al-though there would be some enslavement of Indians until the eigh-teenth century, and there would be Indian tribes in the eighteenth and nineteenth centuries who would own Black slaves.

But Black slavery, meaning Black chattel slavery, viewing Black people as property like any other property (houses, horses, cattle, dogs, fences, and so on), became English colonial slavery and then American slavery. And Black women were at the center of it all: at the center of English colonial history and then the center of Ameri-can history. There were two laws that were passed in the 1660s, first in the Virginia House of Burgess and then in other colonies, that were the basis for establishing black or Black slavery, and that were the foundational laws for all other laws pertaining to Black slavery. The first of these laws, simply put, was that any black slave baptized into the Christian religion could not be eman-cipated from slavery. The second stated, simply put, that any child born to a black slave woman was automatically a slave. And sla-very was a condition of life of generations of slaves, as long as sla-very lasted. The two basic laws and the other laws that followed not only established Black chattel slavery, they legally put Black people at the bottom, first of English colonies and colonial society and then of American history and society. The culture and institutions of the colonies, and the culture and institutions and social life of the new America and American society, functioned to maintain and perpetuate this deep subordinate status of Blacks. In short, Blacks were made the legal and structural bottom, and Black women were made the centerpiece of that, because they produced the Black slave labor, and the Black people who were put in this legal and structural position. This status also applied to nonslave Blacks, because the white supremacy/ebonicism racism as well as the maleist/sexist racism that abetted the establishment of Black chattel slavery helped, along with racist laws and practices and de facto racist practices, to plant and perpetuate them legally, politically, and socially as part of the structural bottom of American society. Thus, more broadly, Black slave women and nonslave women were the centerpiece of the legal and structural subordination of Black people in American national history and society.

This meant, therefore, that the foundation of America, to focus just there, was not the ideals, or culture, or institutions of the country, but Black people, and the culture, social institutions, and social life they established. The Black woman was the center of that, because she reproduced the Black people who did the cultural–social construction, and the Black people who were made the legal and structural bottom of America. Thus, one of the historical roles that Black women played in America, one of the ways they entered and fitted into it, was that they played a major role in reproducing and perpetuating the structural foundation of America; that is, they played a very large role in keeping America alive and ongoing.

From this extremely deep structural bottom position in American history and life, Black women entered into, as a central element, many aspects of that history and life. Owing to the constrictions of space, I'll mention only a few. There was first, and obviously, their entry and place in the American economy. They were critical in producing the generational supply of slave labor that was the primary labor force in the South that produced the agricultural surpluses that brought in revenues, that were in turn used for America's industrial and commercial development. Thus, Black women relate critically to the financial, industrial, and commercial development of America.

Black slave women were critical producers of the property and labor that were used to produce wealth, which both became the means for white men in the South (namely, slaveholders) to dominate southern state governments and southern state and regional politics. They were also a chief means by which other southern slaveholders went to the U.S. government and became senators or representatives, and even presidents and Supreme Court justices. Black slave women produced the people, the slaves, who were described individually as "three-fifths" of a human being, and were the subject of the "three-fifths" clause of the Constitution that was the basis for the critical compromise between powerful northern and southern white men to be able to complete a Constitution and to establish a new national government and a new country. Historian C. Vann Woodward once wrote, "During the greater part of the struggle for power and place and fame that make up so much of American history, black men were kept in chains and illiteracy and subject thereafter to crippling debasement and deprivation. The number of landmarks and monuments they were able to leave on the history of their country was necessarily limited."[35] The only thing limited here was C. Vann Woodward's knowledge of Black history and the role of Black women in that history and in American history. In the first two centuries of America's national existence, Black people were involved in making America the kind of distinctive country it would be, and Black women were at the center of that, because the peculiar way that America became distinctive could not have been done without them.

Finally, Black women became the center of American historical and societal social relationships. Black women, by racist beliefs and practices, by law, and by culture and social institutions, were placed at the very bottom of American society. Their public image was completely disparaged. They were publicly depicted as ugly, coarse, even masculine, and licentious, and because any man was encouraged to have sex with them because of what they might produce, they were also established as the national whore, and had that public image. This was a great and enduring problem for Black women.

But it also presented a problem to white women. They did not wish to be treated like a Black slave woman, or a "nigger wench," so white men had to come up with a different public image of white women, which the latter encouraged them to do and insisted upon. White women were portrayed publicly as the epitome of beauty, graciousness, femininity, and desirability. The contrasting images of the two groups of women that melted to the different lives that they lived and the different places that they had in American history and life, put a barrier between the two groups that essentially precluded an extensive social relationship, and when the latter did occur, it was with the understanding of white women that they were racially and sexually superior to Black women; in short, white women related to Black women on white supremacist/ebonicistic/sexist terms.

White men, because they had to keep an image of white women in their minds as being the epitome of beauty, femininity, gentility, and even chastity, were restrained in the way they had to relate to white women, which meant that there was a restraint on their ability to implement maleist/sexist beliefs and practices against white women. They even found it necessary to concede that white women should have a privileged position with some social power, not so much with respect to them, but with respect to Black women and Black men, so that they could dominate those two elements like they did, and also view it as their right to do so.

White men produced a consequence for white women, placing them on a pedestal. It would contribute to them being placed in a cultural straitjacket and a gender image straitjacket, that would impose an intellectual, psychological, and bodily freeze on them, and even some restraints on their sexuality and liveliness and desirability as sexual beings. But there was the Black woman, whose images as the national whore, as a sexually licentious person, and as a slave to the sexual act were created by white men that stirred up their adrenaline and stoked their sexual urges that induced them to think wildly sexually about Black women or to assault them. After all, a Black woman could not be raped. That was not a concept for white men, nor was it a category of law with respect to Black women. There would be children born between white men and Black women, biracial children of shades of light skin color, but who would be referred to as being Black or black, even in law. Black women were at the center of the creation and perpetuation of the white or light-skinned Black person, who would be regarded as Black or black, but who might "pass" for white, and who in doing this, would escape slavery and the heavy burden of being regarded as Black or black in America. The light-skinned Black person would become the Black person that white people would feel the most comfortable with, the one they could imagine themselves relating to in limited ways and who they might even help in some ways to advance. Light-skinned Black leaders were the ones Whites would feel more comfortable in relating to, and who they would be more willing to help, along with that leader's constituency.

One could go on about the ways Black women have and continue to enter into and fit into America. One way is that they are now in a position to tell the story of Black history and American history in new ways. That process is already underway, and it seems certain that it will be expanded and developed and that this historical writing will produce important things that Blacks and other Americans should know.

Chapter 5

Black History and American Societal Processes

Today there is not much interest in the philosophy of history. In the eighteenth and nineteenth centuries, it had great esteem and importance, as metaphysical philosophers and political and social philosophers and, of course, historians, wrote enthusiastically about the process of European or Western history and the way it was unfolding, and seeing this unfolding following some inexorable patterns or inexorable laws. There was the philosophical view that European or Western history was linear, that it moved from low to high, which meant that it was progressive. This further meant that this history was unfolding in an inevitable way toward greater human development and the full attainment of freedom for all humanity. This was the Enlightenment conception of history, which to its formulators was predicated on the metaphysical foundational belief that human beings were rational in their nature and invested history or the historical process with rational logic and rationality that guided it to its inevitable goals. The fact that Western history and civilization were deeply racist and that this racism acted as fetters on inexorable history was not seen, or was ignored or minimized. The fact that Western history and civilization were promoting the black African slave trade and black African and Black slavery were just seen as encumbrances or aberrations that would be eliminated from view and from that historical process by the continuing inevitable progressive development.

Glib talk or even elaborate talk about the inevitable or inexorable movement of history, or about the inexorable progressive development of human beings and human societies, was brought to an end in Western discourse by an array of impactful things; namely, Hitler, the Nazis, and the holocaustic World War II and the specific Jewish and Slavic holocausts that took place within it; the killer and destructive capacities of science and technology; the urge on the part of Whites/Westerners to hoard or protect the power, prosperity, and wealth they had attained through centuries of wars, racism, colonialism, and imperialism; and the new techniques that Whites/Westerners had devised and were devising to keep the world's peoples subordinate to them and exploitable.

Then the postmodernists came on the scene in the Western world. They unleashed a relentless attack against metaphysical philosophy and philosophies of history predicated on it. They denounced notions of absolute, inevitable, inexorable progress, essentialism, and universalism. They put an emphasis on ideals and values of relativism, difference, pluralism, locality, and localism. This was their subtle way of trying to preserve White/Western hegemony on the planet, to uphold and protect the power, wealth, status, and the distributive power of Whites/Westerners; in short, their way of cloaking their own racism, which was reflected in their concept of modernity (i.e., a modern world), which they claimed was new in history and the world, and that Whites/Westerners had created it and had disseminated it across the globe. They proclaimed themselves postmodernists, seeing modernity as a creation of the Enlightenment and metaphysical thinking. But this did not obscure their racism, except from themselves, in arguing that Whites/Europeans or Whites/Westerners gave the world a modern life, as if modern manifestations of history and life could not be traced all the way back to early human history. The ancient Kemets produced modern features of human existence, and later the Greeks would think of themselves making modern advances beyond the Kemets, with the Romans following them, saying that they had advanced history, culture, and life beyond their predecessors. Later, black Africans and black, white, and brown Arabs, who were all Islamic and who all dominated Spain for centuries, imparted some of their advanced culture to a rather culturally backward Europe by comparison, which was actually the "Age of Enlightenment" of Europe, although that would not be the way the history would be recorded and presented to Europeans, Americans, or other Westerners. The Age of Enlightenment, the historiography repeatedly asserted, occurred in the eighteenth century, and white men brought it forth, and modernity—the modern world—for the first time in human history.

Inasmuch as science, technology, communication, organization, administration, economic productive capacity, and delivery systems were all continuing to expand after World War II, and in a geometric fashion, there was still good reason to talk about human progress and development and the greater development of human societies, even if this was not to be inevitable. It was all practicable with the right kind of politics and economic policies, domestically and globally. Indeed, we had moved into a global age and global history, as historians were now declaring, when things that emerged in one part of the world spread across to other parts with the possible source of origin being anywhere in the world and not just in the Western world.[1] But the postmodernists still talked of relativism, difference, pluralism, and localism, as they invariably said publicly, to accommodate the people outside of the Western world that did not want to be obliterated culturally by the West, showing, in their own minds, how antiracist or unracist they were. But they were reflecting that very same racism by helping to maintain White/Western hegemony on the planet, by doing their part, which was projecting thought that they did not claim to be universal but which they regarded as such, and by writing the new "Great Books," which had previously been written by the "Oldest Dead White Western Males" and making these new postmodern texts of literary standards, knowledge, profundity, and morality the new global texts.

Booker T. Washington had believed in human progress and development, and thus the Enlightenment conception of history, though without its notions of inexorability. He knew very well, as did a number of Black people in his day, how White racism prevented an inexorable movement of history or the inevitable development of human beings and human societies. Du Bois would later argue that the racism of America's white socialists helped greatly to prevent them from being viable, to say nothing about them being a winning political force in the country, and saw that racism making them turn against the progressive history they espoused. Du Bois was not a man of power, but it was his view that there had to be the right kind of ideas to make history progressive and to be able to push it along and to maintain it as a progressive reality. He did not regard ideas as being valid if they were inundated with racism, or analytical methods as being valid or proper if they were interpenetrated by it. Long before Max Weber, Du Bois was calling for "value-free" science or social science. What he meant was the freedom of science beliefs and methods from racist beliefs and values. He unloaded on white social scientists for not making their academic disciplines more scientific, and being able to advance human knowledge with them, because of their racist beliefs and values and the racist fetters on their academic and scientific efforts:

Mentally the blight has fallen on American science. The race problem is not insoluble if the correct answer is sought. It is insoluble if the wrong answer is insisted upon as it has been insisted upon for thrice a hundred years. A very moderate brain can show that two and two is four. But no human ingenuity can make that sum three or five. This American science has long attempted to do. It has made itself the handmaid of a miserable prejudice. In its attempt to justify the treatment of black folk it has repeatedly suppressed evidence, misquoted authority, distorted fact and deliberately lied. It is wonderful that in the very lines of social study, where America should shine, it has done nothing.[2]

Du Bois saw the great difficulty and, in his mind, the futility of Blacks trying to use social science in the heavily racist-inundated atmosphere of his time to try to improve their lives, to push Black history and their own lives along, and to push America along in a progressive, humane manner. He did not abandon science altogether, because he was committed to completing his Atlanta Studies, but in 1905 he became a public agitator and sought to use protest, as a political weapon, to try to free America of the racism that was holding back the development and full freedom of Blacks and America's ability to be and function according to what its ideals dictated.

Booker T. Washington saw a number of things that were required to move Black and American history and history generally along, especially in a progressive manner. It took ideas, power, leadership, organization, communication, and local initiative. By that he meant that people who needed the help the most, as he saw in the case of Blacks in the South, had to take the initiative to help themselves to modernize and develop. Such people needed help in their efforts, and this was where leadership came in, as Washington saw it, and he sent leaders into southern rural areas to help Blacks. The Tuskegean felt that Black people of his day had to make material progress, and a lot of it. Any success they had became initiative, motivation, even a strong desire to make more. Washington theoretically viewed satisfying and expanding material needs as a great motor power of history, and as a method to make history a progressive process. He was also criticized by a number of Black clergy, initially in the South, but then less so there and more so in the North, for emphasizing this materialism and downplaying or ignoring what they called the spiritual side of Black existence. Washington answered such people:

Let us see what is back of this material possession. In the first place the possession of property is an evidence of mental discipline, mental grasp and control. It is an evidence of thrift and industry. It is an evidence of fixedness of character and purpose. It is an evidence of interest in pure and intelligent government.[3]

Washington, with his knowledge of Western history and what he observed happening in America, regarded a middle class as a motor power of history. There was no Black middle class in America, although there were individuals who measured up to those indices. Washington wanted to build a middle class among Blacks, and much of his leadership and programmatic efforts were designed to do that, which was what his northern Black opposition was unable to fathom or did not care about because this was a great fear with them, as it would be taking away their prospective support. Washington used the National Negro Business League to aid in that construction, and also in his efforts to try to link the northern and southern sections of Black middle-class people to build a national Black middle class, which he saw playing a large role in helping to build the national Black ethnic community. With respect to a middle class, he said, theoretically, and applied this theory to Black middle-class people: "They constitute a rather sober, industrious, thrifty, self-respecting group of people, which is the backbone of every race and every people that has successfully entered into and become part of our modern industrial civilization."[4]

Washington was accused by those who thought Blacks should be carrying the struggle directly to white people and seeking to integrate fully into American society, thinking this was the only way to achieve rights and full freedom in the country of promoting a separate Black orientation that they felt would keep Blacks from moving progressively in America during what was felt to be the progressive social, political, and economic atmosphere of the early twentieth century. But Washington mainly led Black people in the South, where there was a very suppressive atmosphere and one of widespread poverty, and it would take more than words of any kind and expressed in any tone to help them move forward. It would take strong leadership, power, organization, and clear materialistic ideas, and that understanding became a strong motivation for Washington to construct the Tuskegee Machine and use it. The Tuskegean felt that it was always power and organization that was at the center of social life and also the great galvanizer of history, especially to make a progressive history and certainly for Blacks in America to make such history.

But Washington was not unmindful of America's lofty ideals. Indeed, he often stated these ideals publicly, and with respect to Blacks, and they were always implicitly involved in whatever he said and did for Blacks. He regarded the materialistic ideas and programs he fostered as simply embodying those ideals, putting flesh on them, as it were. Like so many Black people in America, Washington, while not using the word, which other Blacks did not do as well, felt that there was a *teleological* motion in American history that could be revved up and become a historical momentum. America had lofty ideals—liberty, equality, opportunities, equal opportunities, and justice—which added up ideationally to freedom in the country and the practical fulfillment of that freedom when those ideals were implemented. White racism and White racist power, power that was especially predicated on Black people not being human beings or full human beings, thwarted the teleological movement and unfolding of American history. It was not inevitable history, as Washington and other Blacks saw it, not with white supremacy/ebonicism being the mephitic obstructive force it was in American history and life, impeding America's effort to move progressively and teleologically, according to its own ideals. The Swedish social scientist Gunnar Myrdal would later call this, as indicated by the title of his massive book, *An American Dilemma.*[5] Specifically for Myrdal, the American dilemma, historically and socially, was white people not living up to the ideals of America and engaging in behavior toward Blacks that was contrary to the ideals. What Myrdal did not fathom, and what the Blacks who aided him in his project apparently did not help him understand, was that there was no dilemma in America—which to him was a moral dilemma because white people invested the country's ideals with their racist thinking and racist beliefs, and on this basis used them to suppress Blacks in America, closing down the dilemma and also in a significant way White conscience and morality in the country.

Black people, as a people, have never made history in this country assuming the existence or strength of conscience and morality in white people. They knew where centuries of slavery and racist thinking and practices had left those things. Even Black slaves did not regard stealing from white masters to be immoral. This was a sentiment that Booker T. Washington held, as displayed in a story he told about his mother when she was a slave:

One of my earliest recollections is that of my mother cooking a chicken late at night, and awakening her children for the purpose of feeding them.

How or where she got it I do not know. I presume, however, it was procured from our owner's farm. Some people may call this theft. If such a thing were to happen now, I should condemn it as theft myself. But taking place at the time it did, no one could ever make me believe that my mother was guilty of thieving.[6]

What Washington and other Black people felt they had to do with regard to Whites in advancing in America, which was a long-standing belief among Black people, was to invest conscience and morality in Whites, or help develop or help stiffen what they possessed. Martin Luther King, Jr., built a method of struggle on that understanding. His nonviolent direct action methodology, that took the Black struggle directly to Whites in a nonviolent way, was consciously constructed and implemented to try to invest conscience and morality in southern Whites or strengthen what was already there. These were the purposes for writing his "Letter from a Birmingham Jail," to southern white ministers.

The teleological ideals of America, and a teleological movement of American history based on these ideals, have been traditionally accepted by Black people without much theoretical or philosophical fanfare, and without even knowing or using such words. Without the discourse, they have always accepted the teleological orientation of Black history that derived from America's teleological ideals and history. For Blacks, their teleological history has always been in a push–pull pattern or rhythm; American ideals pulling and Black people themselves pushing, or pushing together with white allies. This was the kind of philosophical view of Black history, that was not woven into a philosophy of Black history that the Black contributionist historians were guided by when they wrote their historical works. As we saw in a previous chapter, historian Robert Harris rejected this as a significant continuing form of Black historiography, although Black women historians are restoring it to a primal place to talk about the contributions of Black women to Black history and American history.

The contributionist historians knew about the separate cultural and social existence of Blacks in America, and the way that Blacks and this life were segregated in the country. They saw their histories that discussed the contributions that Blacks made to America, and the struggle they were making to achieve rights and full freedom in America, as strong ideological attacks against racism and racist segregation; that is, segregation based on the idea that Blacks were "nonhumans" or "subhumans." Historians like Robert Harris, cultural historians or Black nationalist historians as they usually call themselves but whom I call Black ethnic historians because their historiography overwhelmingly focuses on the Black ethnic group and community in America, like to emphasize the separate Black identity and the separate Black history in America.

Actually, Black history has moved on both a separate and integrated basis in American history. These have been the main twin tracks. Blacks had to move on a separate basis, and continually, because White racist power and White racist segregation forced that upon them. They also had continually to move on an integrated basis, because they were compelled by White racism and the teleology of American history and the teleology of their own history to keep moving in this manner, to keep trying to achieve rights, development, and full freedom in the country. Even when Blacks articulate one side of Black history and not the other, they still relate to the other side, always in practice. When the Black Muslims of the 1950s and 1960s were calling for a separate Black country in continental America and were referring to white people as Devils, and were attacking Martin Luther King, Jr., and other leaders they dubbed pejoratively "integrationist leaders," they quietly integrated themselves; for instance, going to schools that were integrated, even if no more than with white teachers and white administrators, and by working in businesses and industries owned by white people. What has always been a problematic thing of Black history and for Black people has been the continuous confusion about the meaning and purposes of certain American societal processes in which they have to participate in America to achieve rights, material progress and development, and full freedom in the country. Blacks are presently at the height of this confusion.

Every society has cultural and social processes that are part of its structure and functioning, in which its inhabitants participate and have to participate to be successful citizens, residents, and successfully make history in the country. The processes overlap each other and form a large web that lays over and interpenetrates the structure of the society. They also have the function of holding it together, integrating geographical regions, and integrating the people of the country who are spread out geographically, drawing them together. People who are minorities in countries, especially despised ones, or those that the society has targeted for oppression or suppression, will find it difficult to gain access to the societal processes and make use of them, with the exception of the one called separation, which they simply cannot be barred from unless they are deported or exterminated. I have mentioned three of these kinds of societal processes already: *separation*, *segregation*, and *integration*. There are also *assimilation* and *acculturation*. There are a number of other of these processes, but these are the ones we will focus on in this chapter to show how Black history has related to them and other societal processes in American history and society. There is another process that will be discussed, which is a very special one, because this is one that Black people created themselves and created for themselves. This is the African Retention process that was created and used mainly in the early existence of Blacks in North America. This process has not been dissolved in Black history or Black life, but it does not function as it once did for Blacks in the country.

Black historians and other kinds of Black intellectuals who talk about "Africanisms" or "African Retentions," invariably have only a reference to the retention of certain black African cultural traits in Black history and life, and usually make it appear that these traits did not become a part of Black culture and Black life, ceasing to be African cultural traits. There are Black and black scholars and other kinds of Black and black intellectuals who, while not thinking of an African Retention cultural process, still think of Black people as being Africans and remaining fully attached to black Africa, living with and developing black African culture in America. I mentioned some of these individuals in the first chapter—Molefi Asante, Maulana Karenga, and Jacob Carruthers, and a number of other leaders and followers. Jacob Carruthers made the following remarks in *Intellectual Warfare*:

Indeed we must take over the education of African people and develop an African-centered curriculum. We also must build the foundation of our renewed educational establishment on the African worldview. We must draw our ideas from the deep well of our heritage. We must build institutions to foster our careers. To this foundation we may add whatever stands the test of truth and prosperity. In other words, we must recreate a universe of African establishments to encompass every phase of life.[7]

Black history, made in the United States and also inside Western history and civilization, which has been happening for hundreds of years, has removed itself and black people and Black life from the African continent and the black people there. Black history is not a part of African history or black African history; that is, it is not black African history away from the continent in another time and place. This is not to say that Black people in this country should not have an interest in black Africa and its peoples, or that they do not have affinities toward them, or that they should not study black African history, especially West and Central African and Kemitic history, or that they should not borrow some black African cultural traits and perhaps even some black African social institutions deemed useful. But Black people can borrow culture from any source and do not have to be limited to black Africa. Any culture that Black people borrow from outside sources will be woven into Black culture and will become a part of it, doubtlessly altered by Blacks to weave in it.

The Africanisms that Black people retained in their early history in America were a basis for creating Black culture and became a part of it, and, as it is known, Africanisms retained usually had to be modified to be of use in the construction. Black people have a primary method of cognition, which I and others have called *diunital cognition*, that will be discussed briefly in this chapter.[8] This was a modification of the cognitive pattern brought to North America. Diunital cognition can deal well with contradictions and complexities and can help Black people develop what I would call a Black-centric Perspective, and even such things as a Black philosophy or a Black philosophy of life that would augment that perspective and that framework for historical and social analysis, and for the construction of social thought including Black feminist or womanist thought.

Du Bois said in *The Souls of Black Folk*, that Black people should not seek to Africanize America, for America has too much to teach the world.[9] He was equally against Black people trying to Africanize themselves and their own lives, which would lead to them trying to Africanize America or consciously withdrawing themselves from American history and society, which he felt would be detrimental to Black people. Two years before he died in West Africa, he said in a speech at the University of Wisconsin,

Today when the African people are arising to settle their problems we are in the peculiar position of being a group of persons of Negro descent who not only cannot help the Africans but in most cases do not want to. Any statement of our desire to develop American Negro culture, to keep our ties with coloured people, to remember our past is being regarded as racism. I, for instance, who have devoted my life to efforts to break down racial barriers am accused of desiring to emphasize differences of race. This has a certain truth about it. As I have said before and I repeat I am not fighting to settle the question of racial equality in America by the process of getting rid of the Negro race; getting rid of black folk, not producing black children, forgetting the slave trade and slavery, and the struggle for emancipation; of forgetting abolition and especially of ignoring the whole cultural history of Africans in the world.

No! What I have been fighting for and am still fighting for is the possibility of black folk and their cultural patterns existing in America without discrimination; and on terms of equality. If we take this attitude we have got to do so consciously and deliberately.[10]

Du Bois's first reference to "African people" was to the black Africans on the African continent, who were engaged in independence struggles. Africans in the world was his reference to black people of black African descent, which he also referred to as "Negro descent," as a number of Black people did at that time, especially Black historians, who could be found all over the world. He regarded Black people as one of those groups of black people who had their own culture that he felt that Blacks in America should preserve and develop, which did not require being antagonistic toward America, withdrawing from America, or rejecting the American identity of Black people. As he said, he was interested in Black culture being equal to other ethnic cultures in America. Du Bois wrote a lot on black Africa and was an early *Africanist*. There have been those who have tried to use Du Bois as a justification for regarding Blacks as black Africans and Black culture as black African culture, but this was never anything that Du Bois advocated, and in his very last years he advocated what he had espoused throughout his long adult life.

Given the kind of historian Du Bois was, a historian generally of the Enlightenment orientation who viewed history as being progressive and forward moving, he would have regarded it as foolhardy for any people, and that would have included Blacks in the United States, to try to make a history that would take them backwards. For Black people to try to become black Africans in thought, culture, and social life, as the proponents of such action want, would be for them to go back in time and space. This is extreme nostalgia, as it is extreme romantic thinking. There is a lot of catching up to Black people, in terms of economic, social, and cultural development, that black Africans have to do; and a number of black Africans know that. There is also the need to catch up to people in the Western world generally in many respects, which is why they come to America or Europe to study, or send their children to do so, expecting or hoping that they will return and put their acquired knowledge and skills to the task of helping their people and their countries to modernize and develop. It has to be said, and sadly, that the black African worldview that Carruthers, Asante, and others champion has not pushed black Africans fast or far, in sizeable aggregate numbers, into the world that people across the world live in, or increasingly live in, and which continues to gallop apace in its development. But there has been more advancement along these lines than these intellectuals realize or acknowledge, because they have a way of talking about black Africans as if they were all still living in quaint villages with thatched huts and deeply enmeshed in their traditional culture and life.

There are a number of Black people in the United States who have to undergo modernization and development in a number of ways, who still show some of the deleterious effects of the ancestral slave and racist-inundated history on thought, personality, social skills, speech, and in other ways. There is no significant Black leadership for that large shackled constituency today, the kind of people whom Washington made his special interest and for whom he provided leadership and programs. But such Blacks and other Blacks in the country are generally hampered in their ability to live in America and to be fully free in the country because those who offer them ideas and leadership show ignorance of or great confusion about some of the critical societal processes of America that Blacks have to be clear about and use effectively. It is really the task of Black scholars and other kinds of intellectuals to provide that clarity for other Blacks, but it has not been forthcoming. In 1962 the Black sociologist E. Franklin Frazier wrote an article talking about the failure of Black intellectuals to provide Black people with adequate intellectual guidance. But Frazier showed himself to be confused about some of America's societal processes, and ones critical to Black people. He showed confusion about assimilation and integration. With respect to the former he said, "Assimilation involves integration into the most intimate phases of the organized social life of a country." He defined integration, saying, "Integration involves the acceptance of Negroes as individuals into the economic organization of American life."[11] As seen, Frazier regarded assimilation and integration to be the same thing in the first remark. In the second he speaks of integration differently, and also in a very limited manner, seeing it as only related to the American economy. Black history, against which both of these concepts can be tested, shows that assimilation and integration are quite different from what Frazier said.

In his book *Blacks and Social Justice*, Black philosopher Bernard Boxill devoted a chapter to the discussion of assimilation and separation, saying that the former had been problematic with Black intellectuals, indicating that some have been in favor of it, others against it, some seeing it as inevitable for Blacks and others seeing it as not something that Blacks have to do or have to avoid.[12] When Boxill discussed separation, he really did not discuss that societal process by that name, but rather by the name of "self-segregation," which, as seen in the chapter on Washington, Du Bois had used. Other people at that time, in the 1930s, used that term, and Blacks used it thereafter. In 1992 Boxill was using it, and many Blacks today still use it. But the term "self-segregation" is wholly inadequate because it does not refer to any kind of process or social reality. The term "separation," which is what is really meant, does. Black intellectuals as well as other intellectuals in America use the concepts of assimilation and acculturation interchangeably, or confuse acculturation with integration. Black history brings great clarity to all these concepts or societal processes, including separation and segregation as part of the contingent, as well as the specialized process of black African Retention, which have all greatly impacted Black history and Black life.

I wish to begin a discussion of these concepts as they have related to Black history and life, with acculturation that affected Black history at its opening. When black Africans came to North America as slaves, they brought their cultural traits with them. But they brought them to a history that was being made that was different, and to an environment that was in many ways physically different from what they had known and that was also very culturally and socially different. They came among a people who thought differently than they, in terms of cognition. The white people they encountered employed several different cognitive systems, where they thought in either–or terms, hierarchical terms, or dualistic terms. The black African slave had what I have called elsewhere a *mono-interactive* form of cognition that involved several forms all rolled into one, which required and enabled them to think in a holistic fashion.[13] This kind of holistic thinking or cognition is still found among the black African people who are descendants of the Africans who became one of the original ancestors of Black people, with the other ancestor being the initial Black people created in North America. The Nigerian intellectual Tejumola Olaniyan describes the traditional kind of black African thinking found in West and Central Africa, which could also be found among other black Africans elsewhere on the continent:

The African worldview, on the other hand, is characteristically thorough and catholic: a relative comprehensiveness of vision in which parts are apprehended in all their fullness, that is, in their dynamic relationships with themselves, in their constitutive identities and parts and wholes. For this worldview, history is not a threat that disperses understanding into unyielding "separatist myths (or 'truths')." On the contrary, new experience, in either harmonious or contradictory relationship to the stock, are absorbed, dealt with, and allocated their proper berths within a vision that resolutely refuses to conceive of life and death, evil and good, heaven and earth, past and present, inside and outside, and so on, as irreconcilable.[14]

This kind of cognition would not be totally destroyed by the black African slave trade, or by Black slavery, or by the new processes in the new social setting, such as assimilation and integration. But all these pressures forced a modification of this form of cognition to hold onto the holistic character as much as possible. But the modification was also part of the acculturation process. This is a cultural process that applies to foreigners or people coming from the outside to a new cultural-social setting to live. It involves two things: shorning or the destruction of original, incoming cultural (and social) traits (although not all of them, just those that are not compatible with the new setting), which occurs over time; and the imbibement of the new cultural and social fare that the incoming people make part of their own.

In the case of the black Africans who came to America to be slaves, the acculturation process was very destructive, but it was not, as it could not have been, totally destructive. Human beings are what their historical, cultural, and social experience have made them. Their cultural and social traits are the bases on which they make history. If the black Africans had been totally denuded of culture and social orientation, as was once said in a strong manner by E. Franklin Frazier and other Black scholars, such as sociologist Charles Johnson and political scientist Ralph Bunche, Jr., virtually all the slaves would have gone insane, because the affects of their minds would have been ripped out. There was great ripping and destruction of cultural and social traits. In places in the South where black African slaves did not have much association with Whites and were slaves in fair numbers, they could hold onto their Africanisms longer. But in time Whites and the new environment of slavery, and the new cultural and social fare, would close in and carry out the acculturation destruction.

Out of necessity, black African slaves held onto their cultural and social Africanness for as long as they could and as much as they could. But they were required to imbibe the new fare, which they could not do extensively because of language barriers, fear (because their masters and other Whites had a fear of them or a strong disliking of them), and for other reasons. Out of sheer human need, black African slaves retained as much of their original culture and sociality as they could. This was the African Retention process, which was mainly a cultural process, and it actually went on for centuries, because black Africans continued to be brought into North America until the 1860s, although in much smaller numbers starting in the early nineteenth century. The new Africans that kept coming in during this time came now into a Black cultural--social world that the Black slaves, the progeny of the original African slaves, were constructing and developing. That new Black culture and social life constituted a creative synthesis. It involved the retention of Africanisms that had to be mixed with the new cultural and social traits of the new environment, English, and other Western traits. The black Africans, as part of the acculturation process, imbibed some of this new fare. The Black slaves, who were born and raised as slaves in North America, assimilated the new culture and sociality, and continued the creative process of synthesizing Africanisms and "Englishisms" and "Westernisms," mixing them together with the slave experience and life as slaves to produce a new Black people of the black race, a new black ethnic group, Black people, who had a culture and social life. This was all aided by the fact that most Black slaves were born in America and did not come from the outside, with encumbering cultural traits and sociality. This facilitated several generations of Black slaves moving into the larger history, culture, and social life around them. This made borrowing from these surroundings easier, assimilating cultural and social fare that went into the construction of Black culture and social life that were the foundations for making a distinct Black history in America. This Black life became the separate societal process that would be a part of Black history to this day.

I want to cut into some of the romanticism that so many Black historians exhibit discussing the retention of Africanisms and Black slave life, and the romantic harmonious image they project of Black slaves, and particularly the image of the harmonious relationship between incoming black African slaves and Black slaves. One reason for the idyllic characterization is that many Black historians do not make a distinction between black African slaves and Black slaves, seeing them all as just African slaves and African people, as they say. The Black slaves, functioning from the separate process, which was a cultural and social process for them (as it is for whoever else used it), were building a new identity, a new cultural–social life, and a workable relationship with their masters and the institution of slavery. The latter was integrally involved in the new identity and existence that Black slaves were creating. When black African slaves came to North America, they eventually came to a constituted Black life, which they saw as being very different from what they knew, and they also experienced rejection by the new Black people. This rejection and conflict, and the Black viewing of black Africans as "foreigners" or "outsiders," is the historical reality that numerous Black historians ignore or obscure to hold onto their view that Black people in America are and have always been Africans.

A former Black slave in the first half of the nineteenth century, George Ball, regarded incoming black African slaves as "foreigners" or "outsiders," and strongly implied that this was a common view held by Black slaves like himself: "The native Africans are revengeful, and unforgiving in their tempers, easily provoked, and cruel in their designs. . . . They feel indignant at the servitude that is imposed upon them and only want power to inflict the most cruel retribution upon their oppressors."[15] This view strongly implies that Black slaves, over their existence in America and in Ball's time, had worked out a relationship of some reciprocity and stability with slavery, and had some space for their own construction initiative and a certain amount of psychological space for an inner peace in relationship to their masters and their bondage. And they did not want incoming slaves, "outsiders," interfering with this situation or wrecking it. Indeed, they were insistent about the Africans coming into the new Black identity and the new cultural–social fold and the new Black history. A former Black slave remarked to an investigator for the oral history project of the Works Progress Administration (WPA) of the Franklin Delano Roosevelt administration, "Most of the time there was more'n three hundred slaves on the plantation. The oldest come right from Africa. My grandmother was one of them. A savage in Africa—a slave in America."[16] Black nationalist historians or Africancentrists, such as Molefi Asante, laud the Gullah people on islands off South Carolina and George, who they use as a source to demonstrate that Africanisms, in this case elements of black African languages, were held onto by Black slaves. Here is what a Black slave said about the Gullah and their manner of speaking: "Somebody give her de name o' Betty, but twern't her right name. Folks couldn't understand a word she say. It was some sort o' gibberish dey call 'Gullah-talk,' and it sounds *dat* funny."[17] There is no friendship, amicability, or harmonious relationship expressed in that comment. Finally, a former slave remarked to an investigator, showing that she regarded herself as being different from black Africans and in reference to her grandmother, "My granny could never speak good as I can. I can't talk no African."[18] The former slaves who talked to WPA investigators were in very late years and were also aware of how the name African was used, although it is doubtful that they heard it used much in their lifetime as slaves. George Ball had heard it, but whether it was Ball or others quoted, the name African generated hostility, not amicability or friendship. That is, Blacks who were directly involved with black Africans seemed to have disliked them and could not really relate to them until they showed the acculturation of Blackness. This was another way the acculturation process worked with black African slaves.

I want now to clarify what the process of assimilation amounts to. This is a cultural–societal process where an individual or a group of people, indigenous to a social setting and born into a community, society, or country, assimilate the cultural–social fare of their indigenous environment, such as ideals, beliefs, values, morality, and normative behavior and internalize them all to make them part of their minds, psyches, and behavior so that they can intellectually, psychologically, and morally participate in the culture and social life of a community, region, or country. Integration is a societal process that means participating in the society. It does not mean equality, and does not necessarily have to be related to equality, because one can integrate or participate in culture, institutions, or social life in an ascendant manner, in a middling manner, or at the lowly bottom. Black slaves integrated into the American economy as slaves, and as unequals. But they also integrated or participated in other social settings that were part of White existence, such as white families where they were servants, or when Black slaves attended White churches. E. Franklin Frazier confined integration to participation in the economic institution. Obviously, assimilation abets integration, because knowing the ideals, beliefs, values, and normative forms of a society or community aids participation.

Let me let Bernard Boxill relate his views of the difficulties that Black intellectuals especially have had with the cultural process of assimilation:

To assimilate, or not to assimilate. To black cultural nationalists, such as the poet Imamu Amiri Baraka (Leroi Jones), as the political theorists Stokely Carmichael and Charles Hamilton, and most important, W. E. B. Du Bois, that has been *the* question in the race issue. Not, of course, that they *imagined* that blacks have had much of a choice about assimilation. Their question was and is about goals. Should the goal be to assimilate, or to become as much like the white majority as possible, to blend in? Or should it be to assimilate, to keep and even to accentuate the differences from the majority to stand out? These thinkers consider that question as crucial and fundamental as Hamlet's. They maintain that to choose assimilation is to choose self-obliteration, to choose, in some important sense, not to be. In their estimation, if black people are not to cave in under the slings and arrows of the majority, they must affirm, maintain, and even accentuate their distinctiveness. But their position has not gone unchallenged. There are black thinkers who have seen nothing crucial in the question of whether or not to assimilate, and no obligation to avoid assimilation. These so-called assimilationists, whose number included Henry Highland Garnet and Frederick Douglass in the 19th century and most of the leadership of the NAACP today, do not say that blacks must necessarily assimilate, though they usually believe that assimilation is inevitable. But they do say that black people are not obliged not to assimilate.[19]

The failure that Black people like the ones that Boxill named and other Blacks have had with the concept of assimilation is that they have not understood what it meant, or have not been able to keep it straight in their minds as to what it meant; or they have let their hostility toward White racism, and also white people, and their desperation to hold onto blackness and Blackness interfere with their ability to understand it and the necessity for Blacks as well as any other Americans to assimilate. There also has always been a confusion exhibited by many Black thinkers about assimilation and *absorption*. The latter is a cultural process that calls for an indigenous group of people to divest themselves of their culture and cultural identity and only accept the general culture and the general identity of a society, community, or region of a country.

This has never really been a problem for Black people, because white people, acting as white supremacists/ebonicists, have never wanted to absorb Black people in America. They would insist on Blacks becoming White culturally (that is, they would project that demand from time to time), but at best they would only be referring to a handful of Black people, fully believing that most Black people were not capable of imbibing or displaying White culture. So this kind of battle about assimilation was always overwhelmingly the battle of some Black intellectuals or some educated Blacks, who also engaged in it because it was a way of resisting white people and fighting back at them—to fight being absorbed—although they might say Black people. After all, they are invariably the only ones who interact with white people that closely and that extensively for this to be a consideration or bone of contention. And still less have Black people had to be afraid of being *amalgamated* in America, or biologically absorbed by the white race in America. But light-skin Black people and Black–White interracial marriage, that some Black people might not like, might induce confusion about assimilation. The American who does not assimilate American culture is seeking not to be an American, or wants great difficulty being an American, and is going to cut off his or her opportunities to acquire or enjoy what Americans can obtain. The goal of Black people in America is to be full Americans and to have full American freedom. Assimilation was never the goal, nor even integration. Assimilation and integration were means to participate in America to pursue American objectives. Separation, the Black separate life, was another means, because this represented collective power that could open up the assimilation and integration processes, as Black people exercising collective Black power in the 1950s and 1960s did.

Separation is the Black separate life in America, and it is not separatism, which more than a few Black intellectuals, including Black historians, have used interchangeably. A distinct ethnic group might well wish to separate from the larger body of people and cultural and social life around them. The American Amish have done that. Only a few Black people over the entire length of Black history have ever been separatists and wanted to withdraw from American society while living in America, or wished to have a separate Black country somewhere on the American continent, or North American continent, or elsewhere in the world, or wished to emigrate from America to a black country to help build it or strengthen it. Black historians regarding themselves as Black nationalist or cultural nationalist historians, and other Black intellectuals regarding themselves as political or cultural nationalists, have blown these two conceptions of Black nationalism into myth and fable, which they made palpable to themselves by referring to Black ethnicity or the Black ethnic group, or the Black ethnic community, as a "nation" or the "Black nation." They are always careful how they phrase this. They know that the word nation is now, as it has been for a long time, juxtaposed to state, and is commonly projected as "nation-state." These kinds of Black intellectuals know—if for no other reason than the few people they know of who think like them—that most Black people do not think of themselves constituting a "nation" or a separate country, or aspire for a separate Black country in America, or wish to emigrate from America. Marcus Garvey learned that lesson emphatically. This is the kind of Black thinking that occurs when the people doing it think of themselves or other Black people as Africans, or have hostility toward white people, or are desperate to hold onto a Black identity or the separate Black life in America. Neither of these things is a real problem for Blacks in America if this is what they want to do. And, in fact, this is what they do during their life in America, and white people do not really try to prevent them, which they could not do anyway. And there are white people who would not even think of trying, because they know that Black aesthetic culture is a commercial pot of gold.

White people have always feared Black people as a collectivity, because they fear Black Power. That is why they have always preferred to segregate Blacks in America. This process involves a group of people forcibly confining another group to a physical, geographical, or social area and keeping them there, contained and controlled. This has been something that Black people have experienced their entire history in America: segregation. But this is not something they have done to themselves, which indicates why "self-segregation" is actually a nonsensical term, referring to no reality whatsoever. Living forcibly confined, forcibly isolated and excluded, Blacks had to develop a separate existence, a separate identity, and a separate cultural and social world, begun during ancestral slavery. White racists have always feared that Blacks might use their separate power to break through segregation, and use that power to make use of other societal processes to open up and pursue opportunities in America to attain full rights and full freedom. Right now Black intellectuals do not think seriously in terms of Black Power anymore, and the White retreat into a greater expression of racism, even if more subtly expressed, has been a consequence of that.

Again, Black people have to use, as do all Americans, the country's assimilation and integration societal processes, and Blacks also have to use the separation process. The three have to be used together, and Black diunital cognition, or Black Cognition, makes that conceptually and ideologically easily possible, because this form of cognition, a modification of the original black African monointeractive cognition, makes it possible for Blacks to deal intellectually and also emotionally with contradictions or complexity. What follows is a brief discussion of what I have come to understand about this form of cognition that is deeply embedded in Black history, culture, and social life, and particularly in Black music, especially the blues, that I have taken from my book *Black Intellectuals*:

Black cognition works in the following manner. Its ideational guidance says that all aspects of reality, whether oppositional or not, similar or different, are individual aspects of reality that have their own properties or dimensions and their own integrity. Even if a given reality has been formed by a mixture of realities (e.g., Black culture), it still is an individual manifestation of reality with its own intrinsicness or integrity. All aspects of reality, while individual, are also equal—equal in the sense that each is individual with its own intrinsic qualities and because all aspects of reality interact with each other on the basis of their intrinsic qualities. This is a manifestation of wholeness in Black Cognition, as realities do not interact with one another except on the basis of their intrinsic qualities, whatever they happen to be, and what can be known of them, and the push is to know as much about the dimensions of a given reality as possible. In Black Cognition, individual realities owing to ideational and psychological attributes and also to diunital organizational logic, are juxtaposed to each other and interact with each other on a horizontal basis. This means that Black Cognition is not vertical cognition, because it does not eruct reality. It is not dualistic cognition because realities interact, and they are not always contradictory. It is not domination– subordination cognition, because the interaction is horizontal and not perpendicular or hierarchal. And it is not dialectical cognition, because there is no overcoming, transcending, or hierarchy, as occurs with this form of cognition. Horizontal interaction of individual realities is the centerpiece of Black Cognition. This keeps individual realities—their intrinsic qualities—in full view. This allows for equal interaction of realities, which is done on the basis of individual intrinsicness or wholeness.[20]

Du Bois clearly recognized the diunital character of Black cognition, or Black Cognition. It appeared in *The Souls of Black Folk*, in an oft-quoted passage of that book that has the phrase, "One ever feels his two-ness,—an American, a Negro." He ends with his view that what Blacks have historically sought in America was "for a man to be both a Negro and an American, without being cursed and spit upon by his fellows, without having the doors of Opportunity closed roughly in his face.[21] Hazel Carby, as she did in *Race Men*, would reject, and rightly so, the word "man" or the phrase "Black man" or "Black men" when they stand for Black people, who have always had women and children as well.[22] But whether talking of Black men, women, or children, one is still talking about Black Americans, who still have the American and Black teleological history upon them, and have to keep moving with and pushing forward by their separate life and by making use of the assimilation and integration societal processes. All of these processes acting in unison, as occurred in the 1950s and 1960s, gives a sizable teleological push.

History is simply not something that happens on its own, that is independent of people, that occurs without them, without them thinking, making decisions, and engaging in actions. It also does not occur outside of societal, cultural, and social processes, which are critical to understand and critical to individuals and collectivities of people to use for personal, social, and historical purposes. This is knowledge that Black people have demonstrated and acted on throughout their history, which has included knowledge of how power related to historical and societal processes. Black history shows, however, that Black intellectuals, leaders, and many other Blacks have also shown considerable confusion about these matters and how to relate to and employ them, which has had negative effects on the abilities and efforts of Blacks to advance in America and to pursue full freedom. Black historians and other kinds of Black intellectuals have to step into this situation with rigorous scholarship and critical commentary to end confusion that exists about processes of history and society so vital to Blacks and their interests and endeavors in America.

Chapter 6

Black History and Black Memory

Today there are Black historians and Black literary figures and artists who are showing an interest in what they call "Black Memory." The most notable of the literary figures is the Pulitzer Prize–winning and Nobel Prize–winning Toni Morrison, arguably the most outstanding literary personage in America today. Recently, Genevieve Fabré and Robert O'Meally published an anthology on the subject of Black Memory, with essays from historians, other kinds of scholars, and literary people, entitled *History and Memory in African-American Culture*. The book displayed the editors' interest in showing how individuals from these three groups seek to fetch things from the Black past that were important and memorable, or that could be made such, and that would then be preserved in the memory of Black people or other people who wished to show affinity or allegiance. As the editors noted, objects of memories, or sites of memory, as they had it, were many:

Whether deliberately or not, individual or group memory selects certain landmarks of the past—places, artworks, dates; persons public or private, well known or obscure, real or imagined—and invests them with symbolic and political significance. Thus a *lieu de memoire* (site of memory) may be a historical or legendary event or figure, a book or an era, a place or an idea.[1]

The editors also made the following important comments:

The writing—narrating—of history has not been the exclusive concern of historians; it has also been the province of artists and writers as well as other thoughtful and sometimes brilliant people. . . . We are thus reminded again that historians are storytellers after all, concerned with introducing characters and shaping their stories with some sense of the rhetoric needed to confront their audience's expectations and to bring the past to life.[2]

The authors of these remarks show their inundation with post-modern thinking, which has had a sizeable impact on historians, and especially literary elements (critics, novelists, or poets) or those who teach these subjects in universities or colleges. Under that influence the authors made some comments with which I take strong exception. Historians do not "introduce" historical figures. They resurrect or reconstruct them. Fiction writers introduce characters, which they make up with their imagination. They even take actual people who have lived at one time and depict them in such a way in their fiction that the people are no longer recognizable as who they really were. The fictionalized character has replaced the real one. The historian is not permitted by the rules of history writing to make up historical figures, historical situations, or historical events. What historians write about are those subjects that can be gleaned from documents or other kinds of extant records. They are not permitted by the rules of historical writing to do with those records whatever they wish; that is, "shape" the historical figures or events any way they wish, rhetoric, metaphors, or tropes to the contrary notwithstanding.

This makes it necessary to say something about the notion of the historian being a "storyteller." This is a staple depiction of postmodern critics of historians and their writing. Many have been very extreme in this depiction, essentially obliterating all concept of history writing, and many historians have submitted to this travesty. They have imbibed down to their sinews the central postmodern thought that nothing exists outside of language, that there is no reality, just language, discourse, or language representations. The following is an example of this submission, by a notable historian, Alan Wildman:

Historians of the present generation are undergoing a remarkable learning process. Heretofore we plied our trade primarily as craftsmen, proud of fully and faithfully reconstituting the past, with little thought for methodological justification or philosophizing. Under an avalanche of influences from outside our discipline we are now obliged to concede that we do indeed construct "narratives," "scripts" that reveal their meaning over time, not unlike novels, and thus are subject to the critical disciplines hitherto

reserved for literature and philosophy. The language and symbolic constructs we use we share with a "cultural field" including fiction, documentary records, personal recollections, and the like—the same words, the
same tropes, the same ideas. . . . If history is narrative, more like a novel
than scientific inquiry, then all "representations" are relative, subjective
and keyed to the cultural demands of the present; all pretense to "objectivity" and dispassion remains just that—pretense.[3]

When the postmodernists initially appeared on the scene they
were mainly literary people, literary theorists or critics, or novelists. They were influenced by the critical theory of the Frankfurt
School of thought and also by analytical philosophy. They denounced
metaphysical philosophy, and then made the strong effort to have
postmodern literary elements replace the philosophers, especially
the metaphysical philosophers, and to have literary theory, or literary or cultural criticism, replace philosophy. Continuing with their
imperial ambitions and activities, they sought to dominate higher
education, especially the humanities and history. People in literary criticism and those who taught literature knuckled under
quickly. Philosophy went under about the same time, with Richard
Rorty leading the capitulation in that area, even going to the extreme of denouncing the word philosophy and philosophy as a subject or body of knowledge. The historians were harder to snare, and
a stronger resistance was put up, but a number went the way of
other scholars and other kinds of intellectuals. Keith Windschuttle
pounced on the postmodernists and the historians who succumbed
to them:

The traditional practice of history is now suffering a potential mortal attack from the rise to academic prominence of a relatively new array of
literary and social theories. As well as making a general frontal assault on
the principles for which the discipline has traditionally stood, these theories have entrenched themselves behind the lines in three specific ways.
First, we are now witnessing a breed of literary critics, literary theorists
and theoretical sociologists who have moved in and begun writing their
own versions of history. To create room for this maneuver they have proclaimed the traditional discipline to be flatly flawed. Second, some of those
who trained as historians and spent most of their working lives in the
field have accepted the validity of the critics' arguments and have written
works from what would once have been regarded as an alien perspective.
In doing so they have been applauded not only by their new allies but by
many who might have been expected to have defended the other side. Third,
there are a small number of very good historians who, though still uphold-
ing the discipline's traditional methodology, have recently incorporated
into their work ideas and practices that a decade ago they would not have
countenanced. The representatives of this last group are embracing assumptions that have the capacity to demolish everything they stand for.[4]

Windschuttle would have some very adverse comments for the editors of *History and Memory in African-American Culture*, very likely rejecting out of hand their view that history is simply "storytelling" and like fictional novels, and that the subject of history was fair game for various kinds of scholars and intellectuals, who would not have to be concerned about observing the canon of history or would argue that there was no such canon. The history canon was a fictional canon, nothing more and nothing less. The Haitian historian and anthropologist Michel-Rolph Trouillot, who could admit to the great difficulties in writing history and ascertaining historical reality and truth, still thinks historians who have succumbed to postmodern thinking have done themselves and history writing a great disservice. He called such historians "constructivists" who write constructivist history: "The constructivist . . . denies the autonomy of the socio-historical process. Taken to its logical end point, constructivism views the historical narrative as one fiction among others."[5]

To be certain, historians have used the historical narrative in ways that have violated the canon and distorted or suppressed historical material and historical reality that should have never been part of their treatment. White male historians, going back to the early lay historians, used the historical narrative to promote nationalistic and patriotic values, and to glorify white men, who were the only people they usually wrote about and who they projected as the only people who had made history in America. The professional white historians who followed them employed the new more scientifically oriented methodology to do the same. And when social history began to move into the ascendancy in the history profession, and when Blacks, white women, and lower-class white people became the subject of historiography, the old white male historical guard was livid and regretful. One of them, Thomas Bailey, remarked in the late 1960s, "Pressure-group history of any kind is deplorable, especially when significant white men are bumped to make room for much less significant black men in the interests of social harmony."[6] Even Louis Harlan was smitten by the white male old-guard reaction bug. Speaking before the Southern Historical Association in 1960 about the vast writing in social history and about the neglected or obscured American historical subjects, he remarked, "The historical profession has to pay for these gains, however, by some losses. The faith or illusion of balance and objectivity in our scholarship and discourse has lost ground to racial, sexual, or ideological polemics."[7]

Postmodern critics would not be concerned to lodge criticism of Bailey's and Harlan's remarks, except in passing. The postmodernists helped to inspire social historians, and helped this kind of historiography to develop as it has. As seen, some historians have been smitten by postmodern thinking. But the postmodernists were anxious to dominate historians and other academics and have all of them accept their basic philosophical thought, which was their a priori foundational thought, which they did not endeavor to sink deep into philosophical soil, that there was no such thing as reality. Thus, there was no historical reality, just language representations. This would be asking Black people, for instance, to believe that America never had slaves, just a "discourse" about slavery, that their ancestors in America were not slaves, just some linguistic "representations," or that Black people were not lynched, burned at the stake, or in other ways murdered by white racists between the 1880s and 1920s, and even thereafter, that these were simply manifestations of "word games."

As seen, Black people had been victims of racist "representations," "racist discourse," and racist "word games" for a long time, and also victims of racist "truth regimes," as Michel Foucault would have said, and "social construction" of "race," and knew about all of this and wrote about all of this, although they did not have the language or concepts that the postmodernists devised at a much later date. The development of Black lay history writing and the professional Black history writing that followed both had the objective of attacking and rejecting, directly and indirectly, the White racist "representations," "social constructions," and racist "depictions" of Black people by white historians, such as Ulrich Phillips, or the Dunning School of American historiography; in short, attacking and rejecting the racist "truth regime" of the history profession. W.E.B. Du Bois pounced on it in 1935 in the essay he wrote at the end of *Black Reconstruction* entitled "The Propaganda of History," in which he said,

Assuming, therefore, as axiomatic the endless inferiority of the Negro race, these newer historians, mostly Southerners, some Northerners who deeply sympathized with the South, misinterpreted, distorted, even deliberately ignored any fact that challenged or contradicted this assumption. If the Negro was admittedly sub-human, what need to waste time delving into his Reconstruction history . . . in propaganda against the Negro since emancipation in this land, we face one of the most stupendous efforts the world ever saw to discredit human beings, an effort involving universities, science, social life and religion.[8]

One can see things like the postmodern "linguistic turn," and the postmodern "representations," "word games," and "discourse," in Du Bois's remarks. But the Black scholar would be using these phrases differently than the postmodernists. The latter used them and argued that they were simply abstractions, because there was no reality to relate to. Du Bois would have said there was the historical reality. White historians just sought to deny it, ignore it, and diminish it, and even to make up some other fanciful, perverse "social constructions" regarding Blacks after the mid-nineteenth-century war.

But after saying all this it is still necessary to be clear about what historians are supposed to do, that rules for researching and writing history require them to do, which they might well violate carrying out these objectives and which might draw appropriate criticism. But the rules of researching and writing history distinguish this discipline from fiction writing and the rules of doing that, marking them off clearly as two different forms of human literary effort. Constructivist historians either did not fully understand the rules of the history canon or simply forgot them. It may also be that they confused the two sets of rules, but in favor of the postmodernist point of view.

This brings us to the need to consider three different things to further this discussion. The first is the *silences* of history, then the matter of *truth and history*, followed by a discussion of the *philosophical principle* on which history writing and art, generically considered, are conducted, which clearly distinguishes them conceptually. A problem that always plagues history writing is that historical evidence is often scant, or it can be difficult to come by, as when archives are closed, or the evidence might be overflowing and all of it cannot be considered to write on the subject, which leaves something out of the discussion. These kinds of problems invariably lead to silences in history writing; that is, things are not included or fully included, or are omitted. This is the sine qua non of writing history, even when one is trying to be very professional about doing so. Michel-Rolph Trouillot said the following about the silences in history writing:

Silences enter the process of historical production at four crucial moments: the moment of fact creation (the making of *sources*); the moment of the assembly (the making of *archives*); the moment of fact retrieval (the making of *narratives*); and the moment of retrospective significance (the making of *history* in the final instance).[9]

The silences that appear in history writing in no way occlude the understanding that a historical reality or realities have occurred. Nor do they point, in a necessary way, to the interest of a historian to diminish, distort, or suppress history and historical understanding. There could just be the problem of inadequate evidence, or evidence that cannot be authenticated for its inclusion. But there are other reasons for silences in history writing that are related to the best professional efforts to write history. Historians, like other people in academia, are specialized in their subjects and in their methodologies. But in academia, a given academic area spawns subspecialists, and these can subdivide even further. The divisions might well engender numerous methodologies. In history, there are political historians, cultural historians, intellectual historians, social historians, military historians, urban historians, oral historians, and so on, with similarities and differences in methodology. This kind of specialization and fragmentation in professional history writing makes it difficult at best for a historian to think of anything other than a small piece of any period of historical reality, and to write on such a narrow subject, which makes historical silences unavoidable. Students in pursuit of Ph.D. degrees in history (or any academic area) are told to research and write on some minute topic. The writing of a dissertation is based on a theme that pertains to the subject, and an important part of writing a dissertation is to employ evidence and narrative to validate the theme. Then there is the monographic approach to writing history, which reinforces the specialization and fragmentation of the discipline and reinforces the inevitability of some silences in historiography.

There is also the matter of historical truth, which is greatly affected by thematic writing and specialization and fragmentation. Historians normally do not seek the whole truth about a historical subject, even if reams of evidence were available to try to attempt that rendering. Historians are trained and encouraged to find their small truth and to try to verify it with evidence. So the appropriate way of looking at history writing and truth is to understand that historians, as professionals, and in terms of the craft and its professional function, seek to search out and verify as much as evidence and critical interpretation makes possible, a dimension or dimensions of truth, which can vary in extent or size depending upon the subject of investigation and what is said about it. The pursuit of the large truth or the whole truth (which is never possible) is the work of historical synthesis, which is only rarely done in professional history writing.

The critical interpretation of evidence and subject matter is not purely subjective in history writing, as the postmodern critics contend. Even physical or natural scientists interpret evidence to set up hypotheses, to experiment, and then to clarify the meaning of data or the results of experiments. Physical and natural scientists gave up the notion of strict determinism, or positivism, or objectivity, when they noted the reality of indeterminism, relativity, and complementarity in the phenomena they studied. Historical evidence or facts do not necessarily speak for themselves. They often do, and clearly, such as a birthdate of a historical figure, or the person's death. But the reality of a social change is not always discernible, and it is necessary to try to give it as much clarity as possible, which requires evidence, critical analytical skills, and interpretation. There is a scientific procedure, and this and other features constitute the scientific capacity of history writing. There is also a literary dimension to history writing that in itself is nonscientific, but it is not art, as even some historians have been inclined to say. Historians do use literary devices such as metaphors, tropes, or rhetoric when they write history. A dissertation or a monograph might be organized around a metaphor or a trope, but the historian has the professional and canonical obligation to find the evidence to verify and to support that metaphor or trope.

This brings us to the final matter of the philosophical principles on which history writing and fiction writing and art generally are done. The former, in terms of the obligation of the craft, functions from the premise of *liberty*, while the latter functions from the principle of *license*. Liberty or freedom means that an individual can do some things but not others, because to do the others would infringe upon someone else's liberty. Artists of any kind operate on the principle that they are under no canonical or other restraints and that they can do as they please regardless of what anybody else thinks or feels about it. It is not their concern, no matter how anyone feels about what they render. The Black poet Langston Hughes wrote in 1926,

We younger Negro artists who create now intend to express our individual dark-skinned selves without fear or shame. If white people are pleased we are glad. If they are not, it doesn't matter. We know we are beautiful. And ugly too. The tom-tom cries and the tom-tom laughs. If colored people are pleased we are glad. If they aren't, their displeasure doesn't matter either. We build our temples for tomorrow, strong as we know how, and we stand on top of the mountain free within ourselves.[10]

Langston Hughes regarded license to be the same as freedom. This is also true of Toni Morrison, who regards this as the understanding of all fiction writers:

Fiction, by definition, is distinct from fact. Presumably it's the product of the imagination—invention—and it claims the freedom to dispense with "what really happened," or where it really happened, or when it really happened, and nothing in it needs to be publicly verifiable, although much in it can be verified. By contrast, the scholarship of the biographer and the literary critic [she does not mention historians] seems to us only trustworthy when the events of fiction can be traced to some publicly verifiable fact.[11]

The difference between history and fiction writing or art generally was stated here very clearly. But why does this clarity not even significantly obtain in American culture? Because American history, culture, and social life have always conveyed more strongly than any other understanding that liberty or freedom was the same as license, without using the word license. Artists, when confronted with censorship or efforts to block presentation of or to bar their art, argue their resistance from the premise of the First Amendment to the Constitution, which reads in part, "Congress shall make no law . . . abridging the freedom of speech." The amendment says nothing about the executive branch of the government or the Supreme Court or any government in the United States or any judicial body doing this, although Supreme Court and other court rulings have entered the picture to prohibit governmental and judicial bodies from doing so.

But there is a hidden dimension to the First Amendment with regard to the matter of freedom of speech. The Founding Fathers, to a man, believed that liberty or freedom was the same as license, and this was particularly true of the thirty-odd slaveholders, including George Washington, James Madison, and James Monroe, who helped to construct the Constitution and the new federal system of government. These particular Founding Fathers, and others like them, were violating the rights and freedom of people every single day, and there were other members of the Constitutional Convention who accepted this violation as being natural and appropriate. They would not have liked to have been made slaves themselves and have been dominated, suppressed, controlled, violated, and exploited, constricted in their physical movements, greatly suppressed socially, and prevented from speaking in any public way against the people who were doing this to them or about their condition.

Many of the Founding Fathers owned Black slaves or were establishing a new government that would sanction Black slavery, even though this would be done in coded words and phrases in the Constitution. The Founding Fathers, those who were slaveholders or otherwise, were certainly not interested in the freedom of speech of Black slaves. So they knew that when they inserted that clause in the First Amendment, it was not something that was universally applicable as far as they were concerned, and they were not going to let it be. Black people as slaves in particular, but also nonslave Blacks, were not to have the same rights as Whites in America. Slaveholders wanted to be able to talk to Black slaves any way they wanted to. They owned them and felt they had a right to do that. Other Founding Fathers were in full agreement with that, as they and other white people in the new United States were greatly dependent upon Black slave labor and the fruits of that labor.

The Founding Fathers accepted the fact that slaveholders could buy and sell their slaves, whip them, and, thus, be abusive to them. They accepted the fact that they had a right, even a right publicly, to chastise them, to disparage their intellectual abilities, to castigate their character, to belittle their feelings, to insult them, to humiliate them, and to shame them. These were their rights, their freedom, and it was all *pure license*. But it was not called that or understood as that. It was called and understood to be freedom; namely, freedom of speech. Slave-holding and nonslave-holding Founding Fathers regarded a private and public psychological assault against Black slaves as an important way to maintain them as slaves. Attacking their self-esteem, their self-respect, humiliating them, was a means, they all believed and accepted, to weaken their rebellious spirit and to make them more compliant as chattel slaves.

So this right, this peculiar right of freedom of speech to be publicly abusive to people, this licentious form of behavior, could not be abridged by the men at the Constitutional Convention, constructing a document of political principles and establishing a new government. Black slavery, the first form of Black bondage, lasted 230 years, which meant that for 230 years white people, first in the English colonies and then in America, had a right, verbally or in writing, to be publicly abusive to Black people, which was called freedom of speech. The Constitution had provisions against physical abuse, as one amendment said, against "cruel and unusual punishment." But this was a reference only to physical abuse and not psychological abuse. The Constitution was silent on psychological abuse, just as it was silent about Black slavery. But the ability to engage in public psychological abuse was in the Constitution, understood by the Founding Fathers to be ensconced in and legitimized by the First Amendment to the document that could not be abridged by the Congress. Other Whites would not want this amendment or right abridged either, because they wanted to be able publicly, in verbal or written ways, to abuse Black people, seeing it as an important means to keep the two races separate, to keep white women from Black men, reinforced by antimiscegenation and castration laws, and to keep Blacks in their extreme low station in America. And then there was racism itself, namely, white supremacy/ ebonicism (but other forms of racism as well) that said, as a pure licentious concept, that human beings were not human beings, or not fully so, and could be dealt with any way the racist found it satisfying. All racist social practices by individuals, groups of people, or institutions were licentious behavior. Frederick Douglass understood this very well. In a famous Fourth of July speech in the 1850s, he said,

What, to the American slave, is your 4th of July? I answer; a day that reveals to him, more than all other days in the year, the gross injustice and cruelty to which he is the constant victim. To him, your celebration is a sham; your boasted liberty, an unholy license . . . your shouts of liberty and equality hollow mockery.[12]

The license of white people was invested in them, especially by white supremacy/ebonicism and its practices, and also by promoting and/or sanctioning Black chattel slavery and by perpetuating all these things. Northern and southern white people engaged in licentious behavior toward Blacks wherever they encountered them in the culture, institutions, or social settings in America. Thus, it was deeply rooted in American history, culture, and social life, and it was always understood by Whites to be their right, an expression of their freedom. Their right or freedom to talk or write about Blacks publicly any way they wished was legitimized by the First Amendment. They could also treat Blacks, slave or nonslave, any way they wished. Slave laws and racist "black laws" legitimized and encouraged that. The concept of "the rule of law" in America was predicated on racism and licentious behavior.

So it has not just been artists in America who have believed that license was the same as liberty or freedom, that verbal or written abuse was the same as freedom of expression, and that all of this kind of behavior, the psychological abuse or assault against people, was protected by the Constitution. This was the general understanding of white people in the United States, passed onto one generation of Whites after another through the culture, which was inundated at all times with white supremacy/ebonicism racism that was continually invested in white people, and not just in early childhood or youthful years, but throughout their entire lives.

White male historians showed their racist endowment when they wrote American history and consciously and unconsciously *invisibilized* Blacks in American history in textbooks, monographs, or syntheses. They showed the same behavior toward white women in their writings. The canon called for them to operate from the principle of freedom, to keep in mind that there were things they could do in writing history but other things they could not do. They could not falsify evidence, they could not make up facts or evidence, they could not write about historical situations, individuals, episodes, or events in their written works that had not occurred. There was the canonical requirement about truth, a truth that had to be based on evidence and could not be made up. There were many violations of the canon, which would not have been a concern of fiction writers or artists. Toni Morrison, in an essay titled "The Site of Memory," printed in a collection titled *Inventing Truth*, remarked,

> For me—a writer in the last quarter of the twentieth century, not much more than a hundred years after Emancipation, a writer who is black and a woman—the exercise is very different. My job becomes how to rip that veil drawn over "proceedings too terrible to relate." The exercise is also critical for any person who is black, or who belongs to any marginalized category, for historically, we were seldom invited to participate in the discourse even when we were its topic.

> Moving that veil aside requires, therefore, certain things. First of all, I must trust my own recollections. I must also depend upon the recollections of others. Thus memory weighs heavily in what I write, in how I begin and in what I find significant. Zora Neale Hurston said, "Like the dead—seeming cold rocks, I have memories within me that came out of the material that went to make me." These "memories within" are the subsoil of my work. But memories and recollections won't give me total access to the unwritten interior life of these people. Only the act of imagination can help me.[13]

Only the act of imagination can help is the same as saying that a writer can write on the interior life any way they wish—of a fictional character, not an actual human being, which could well bring slander or libel laws into the picture. A historian cannot deal with the interior life of a historical figure unless the evaluation is predicated on evidence. Psychological or sociological theory would not be enough, as Stanley Elkins found out with his book *Slavery*.[14] The main developer of fictional characters, fictional situations, or a fictional world is the power of the writer's imagination and ability to use words, particularly descriptive language. Morrison asserted that her own kind of writing, and she would accept this as being the case with other fiction writers, "yield[s] up a kind of truth." But does it? Can truth be something that does not exist, that has never happened, that cannot be verified by any kind of tangible thing, not even the senses? The truth about a pink flying elephant, or a fifty-foot giant in a novel, would be what? These could be metaphors, standing for something symbolic and thus meaning something. And I think that what the fiction writer and other artists are more concerned about is meaning or a moral. But a historian is obligated by professional writing to be concerned about truth, the actual, and evidence to reveal it and substantiate it; that is, to reconstruct it and authenticate it.

Historians have used their written works to create and to project myths, and have also used historical methods and evidence, in violation of the demands of the craft, to create and project these things. They, like fiction writers or other artists, such as poets, painters, or dramatists, realize the power of myths, the political value and functioning of myths, and the meanings that can be conveyed by myths. There is the overriding myth and legend of Abraham Lincoln in American historical writing, at the hands of white historians mainly, although some Black historians have contributed to that myth and legend. Benjamin Quarles once wrote that Lincoln did not harbor any racist thoughts and feelings against Blacks, and even said that he was "a man without bigotry of any kind." Then he said, in a contradictory manner, that Lincoln "was no advocate of Negro equality," and that Lincoln did regard the Negro "as inferior."[15] It is hard to account for such a glaring dichotomy. Quarles obviously wanted to say something critical about Lincoln, but he also apparently felt a need, consciously or unconsciously, to bend to the Lincoln myth and legend. John Hope Franklin once wrote, "Few had suffered during the war years more than Abraham Lincoln."[16]

One can imagine a very large number of Black people suffering as much as if not more than Lincoln. Frederick Douglass had no patience for the Lincoln myth and legend being constructed in his lifetime. In a speech in Rochester, New York, at a ceremony to honor Lincoln with a monument, the Black abolitionist remarked, "In his interests, in his associates, in his habits of thought, and in his prejudices, he was a white man. . . . He was preeminently the white man's President, entirely devoted to the welfare of white men."[17] The Lincoln myth and legend are metaphors of American history for application and arousal of white people. They do not represent a memory site for Black people, and, indeed, stand as metaphors of Black oppression or suppression. It always has to be remembered that Lincoln's ideal program for Blacks was to colonize them or deport them—all, slave and nonslave, 4,500,000 Black people—from the United States. Historian David Donald said the following:

Lincoln's persistent advocacy of colonization served as an unconscious purpose of preventing him from thinking too much about a problem that he found insoluble. . . . For a man with a growing sense of urgency about abolishing, or at least limiting, slavery, who had no solution to the problem and no political outlet for making his feelings known, colonization offered a very useful escape.[18]

Historian Nathan Huggins took up an interest in myth even though he knew and even said that history writing and myth were not an appropriate mix. Nevertheless, he felt compelled to plunge his scholarship into that synthetic maze:

In 1971, I was inclined to dismiss myth as not the proper work of historians. Although I still believe that professional historians have a responsibility not to pander to primal emotional needs and fantasies, I have come to appreciate better how the mythic can suggest itself into the most scholarly work. We blacks writing Afro-American history, no matter how much distance we like to maintain, are drawn to "tell the story of our people" in epic scale.[19]

And Hugging also said:

Vincent Harding's *There Is a River* and my own *Black Odyssey* are works driven by such need. There are many differences between these two works: differences in scale, in vision, in sense of history. Yet the similarities are noteworthy: their literary character, and the use of literary devices to insinuate oneself and one's ideas into the experience of both the subject and the reader. Both attempt to include the reader in the *we* of the history. These are not *they* and *me* books. *We* and *our* are the dominant (though often implied) pronouns: we as Afro-Americans, we as slaves.

They are similar in another way: Each has a dominant theme making the book cohere. That theme is explicit and relentless in Harding's work. In my own it is implicit, but nonetheless deliberate and obvious. Harding tells the story of black Americans as a story of resistance, with the "river" of resistance being the central metaphor. For my part I make the slave experience one of transcendence of tyranny. The themes are not only narrative devices, they are instruments of historical selection and interpretation. The strokes are broad, antithesis muted or denied. In short, both works are attempts at epic.[20]

Huggins used the phrase "historical selection" to describe what he and Harding did. Historians are always selecting, presenting, and developing themes of chosen historical subjects. But when a single theme stands for the entirety of a people's or a country's history, this can only be regarded as having some affinity to the old positivistic notion of monocausation. In the case of these historians, there is a much stronger affinity with romantic thinking and the construction of romantic images of a historical group. Harding left out of his book that large and obvious strand of Black history that shows where Blacks, owing to their oppressed condition and not having much choice, abetted their own oppression and often cooperated with oppressors. And there was also a wrinkle on that, engaging in abetting and cooperation as a means to mitigate oppression and to carve out more space within the context of oppression for intellectual, psychological, moral, and spiritual autonomy. This all constituted Huggins's view of Black slave "transcendence of tyranny." But this metaphor and efforts to support it suppresses the fact, and consideration of the fact, that the Black body did not transcend slavery and the domination and abuse of slavery, and how Black slaves, to protect their bodies as much as they could, abetted and cooperated with slavery in ways that could offer that protection.

Historical Black resistance and historical Black transcendence are easily historical memory sites for Black people, but the way Huggins and Harding dug into each of these sites violated the historical canon in a significant manner. They created, in each instance and considerably, a fanciful view of Black history that left it open to critical attack as historical scholarship, which they both experienced. I myself like more latitude in writing history than the history canon allows, the way it is presently constituted. I like more room to use various kinds of devices, literary ones, some philosophy, and psychological, social, and cultural analyses. I mainly write historical sociology or social science history. But there is still the matter of evidence and also historical reality and historical truth. I happen to think that it takes more than standard historical writing to get at these matters and to render them as fully as possible.

It seems obvious that this is not something that fiction writers or other kinds of artists can do if they follow the philosophical principle that guides their thinking, motivation, and work. Some people seem to think that historical novelists and historical novels can do this. One of them is Jane Campbell, who thinks that historical novels can portray historical truths, but who in making this assertion argues quite to the contrary and shows the actual threat that historical fiction can present to history and historical truth:

For Afro-American writers, whose ancestors were wrenched from their native country, enslaved, and forced to subscribe to damaging notions about themselves and their heritage, the creation of a distinct mythology has been almost essential to the artists' process. Afro-American historical fiction from William Wells Brown's *Clotel* (1853) to David Bradley's *Chaneysville Incident* (1981), has fused history and myth into a new reality that enshrines blacks' efforts to maintain their humanity despite the forces acting on them. Idealism pervades black historical fiction. Writers insist on heroism, even when such heroism seems inaccessible in everyday life. That mythic transcendence continually preoccupied black men and women wishing to convey historical truths should not be surprising, given black literature's serious purposes, among them the countering of dehumanizing images imposed for generations. For, as Darwin T. Turner remarks "a confident people must . . . have a transcendent vision of what might be, a vision drawn not only from their triumph but even their despair."

Because the black artists invariably write from an intensely political perspective, he or she searches for rhetorical devices that will move the audience on the deepest level. Myths, by definition, voice a culture's most profound perceptions, and when given fictional form, can awaken an audience's strongest impulses. Thus black writers who rely on myth have the potential to provoke whatever responses they wish: to move the audience to consciousness, to attitude, even perhaps to action.[21]

Campbell shows very clearly why historical fiction or any fiction cannot be equated with historical writing and the rendering of historical reality or historical truth. She showed very clearly that historical novelists, like other fiction writers, do their work on the philosophical premise of artistic license to be able to write on a subject, even something understood as a historical subject, such as the *Chaneysville Incident*, any way they wish, irrespective of historical evidence, historical reality, or historical truth. And the fact that Black writers and literature have "serious purposes" does not mean that that literature, fiction, drama, short stories, or poetry is concerned with truth or dealing with truth. In most instances it is a focus on what literary and other artistic people are concerned to focus on, meaning and moral, and, it also has to be said, to arouse emotion. What historical novelists in particular do is to construct, with imagination and language, and sometimes historical evidence, imagined historical figures, episodes, events, or settings. They then seek, through literary devices, to embody the imaginings, to make them appear real, as if they were things that once existed or happened. But this is all illusion, fantasy, fiction. Historical novelists do not write history. Imaginary people, events, or settings cannot be verified, which is always a historian's obligation.

On the other hand, I am not saying that fiction writers or artists should not deal with myth or convert historical sites or historical memory sites into myths, because it is legitimized by the philosophical principle from which they operate. This principle legitimizes picking out Black historical memory sites and romanticizing and mythologizing them, and also projecting meanings and morals with them, and arousing thought and emotion, usually not with the caution that the wrong thought or emotion or political or social response might be engendered. This is not something that such people will perhaps be significantly concerned about, because they operate on a principle of no restraints in their artistic activity, which carries over to their political and social thinking, helping to stimulate them, and even, sometimes, making them feel messianic.

But it has to be of serious concern to Black historians what Black artists do with Black history or Black historical memory sites. Black

historians have not always shown great concern for them themselves, because they have written on them with a lot of artistic
motivation. Much of the writing on antebellum Black chattel slavery by Black historians has an idyllic aura, a mythical projection
of Black existence during this slavery. What myth does is to suppress or cover up reality, because it is not particularly concerned
with it, or historical truth. An idyllic view of Black slavery by historians or artists that eliminates the oppressiveness of that life for
Blacks will not be a helpful explanation for the millions of Blacks
who are still showing disabilities significantly related to those centuries of great oppression. Romanticizing and mythologizing that
experience might be soothing and might evoke emotional or imagin-
atory transcendence, but it will not lead to empowerment, liberation, or development of millions of Blacks still suffering significantly
from the ancestral afflictions. It may all make for good fiction, good
drama, or good poetry, and also lead to promotions, higher sala-
ries, or royalties, but the lot of Black people who need great help,
and who have been momentarily emotionally lifted, will be the same.

There is also the fact, which has to be of concern to Black historians, that there are some plain and simple false historical memory
sites that Black historians and Black artists both like to evoke,
and which they project in their works and erect fanciful images
and myths about. The names African and African American, or the
view that Black culture in America has always been and continues
to be black African culture, are false historical memory sites. The
notion of a Black nation is a false site, never having any embodiment in Black history or American history. It has always been an
abstract idea of a few individuals over the entire history of Black
people, and it was often used erroneously, often employed synony-
mously with race, ethnic group, or ethnic community. Cultural nationalism, as Black history shows, is a nonexistent situation, and
represents, again, some abstract thinking of a few Black people.
Madhu Dubey devoted her book, *Black Women Novelists*, as she
said, to the "black cultural nationalism" theme found in the writing of Black women writers, when all of these writers, in fact, wrote
about Black ethnicity and the Black ethnic community.[22] Black
women historian of Black women's history Deborah Gray White
titled the opening chapter of her recent book *Too Heavy a Load*,
"The First Step in Nation-Making."[23] But nowhere in her book did
she discuss Blacks trying to build a country in continental America
or elsewhere in the world.

There is another peculiar kind of false history and false historical memory site that Black historians and Black literary people
especially conjure up, and which also amounts to falling for and

thus elevating a debilitating myth for Black people that actually is a myth that white people have devised for Blacks that Black intellectuals and other Blacks have taken over and made their own, much like Whites have wanted them to. This is the myth of Blacks being simply and only a minority in America, or simply and only a "marginalized" people in the country's history, culture, and social life. Toni Morrison said, as will be recalled, that Blacks in America belonged to a "marginalized category," and "historically . . . were seldom invited to participate in the discourse even when we were its topic."

These comments were not elaborated on by Morrison, but left hanging, and in that mold conveyed the impression that Black people were "outside" of historical happenings or historical significance in American history and life and that Blacks had no impact, or were not capable of making an impact, on decisions that Whites functioning as racists and as the majority population made about them. Actually, Morrison would recognize the exaggerated character of her comment on marginalization, because in other writings she evidences a flexibility in understanding and employing this term. In *Playing in the Dark*, for instance, she showed how the "marginalized presence" of Blacks in America had a powerful indirect impact on White fiction writers and the way they wrote about white people and America.[24] The question comes down to, as just implied, Black writers having to recognize when it is appropriate to use terms like minority, marginalized, or even invisibilized with respect to the Black reality and Black experience in America, as Blacks often loom larger than these designations and stations in America.

Blacks have always been a numerical minority in America compared to Whites, although at one time, in 1776, when the American population was 2,000,000 people, 500,000 of that number were Black people, mainly as slaves. In many slave states Blacks were a very large minority, and the majority of the population in South Carolina during slavery. On slave plantations where Whites were also found, Blacks were clearly in the majority. In the "Black Belt" of the South in the late nineteenth and early twentieth centuries, Blacks constituted a very large part of the population of that collection of southern states. Today, there are many cities where Blacks are the majority of the population. Yet the dominant minority image persists, as well as the dominant image of Blacks being "marginalized" or still being "less than" in America, particularly in terms of contributions to this country's history, culture, and social life. Unfortunately, the image of being a minority still grips the thought, perception, and imagination of most Blacks and the image they have of themselves, which carries debilitating effects.

In fact, as Black history and American history show, Black people, as a minority population, have had an enormous impact on American history, culture, and social life. I indicated the impact of Black women. Black men could have also been included in the discussion of how Black slaves contributed to the economy, politics, and social life, first of the British colonies, and then of America. The Black contribution along these lines to early America has become the subject of increasing research and extensive publication, such as Mechal Sobel's *The World They Made Together* and William Piersen's *Black Legacy*.[25] Black people and white people in the South, from slavery on, had an impact on each other as to the way each spoke English. What is called "southern culture" has been strongly influenced by Black people, going back to the origins of slavery. Blacks as a minority played a critical role in the U.S. victory over the Southern Confederacy, and Lincoln had to admit that he and U.S. forces could not have won the war without them. Blacks did not play a direct part in the decisions that ended Black chattel slavery, but they engaged in actions that had a great bearing on those decisions. In the 1950s and 1960s there were not many Black people sitting in Congress, but the decisions that Whites made in that institution would not have been made at all if Blacks had not put pressure in an acute manner on such people to make decisions, many favorable to them and America.

When Blacks make progress many Whites automatically come in for benefits, making advances or gaining benefits by riding the progressive or rebellious "coattails" of Blacks. The "War on Poverty" to help Black people could not possibly have been passed in Congress unless it was a war that was to be extended to lower-class Whites. The Black Liberation Struggle of the 1950s and 1960s brought gains for white women and even the white female feminist movement, for disabled or physically challenged Americans, and for Jews and other Americans who suffered from civil disabilities, and it also opened the door to give serious consideration to the rights of children. One only has to mention the impact of Blacks on American sports to realize the enormity of that contribution; or music, or dance, or on spoken English in the country, and now, and increasingly, American literature and other letters. The novelist and essayist Ralph Ellison devised what he called his "Ellison law" that related to Black history and American history and life: "First something happens to us; and then, just wait, it happens to every other group in America."[26] The editors of *History and Memory in African American Culture* wrote the following:

The black something that happens can be a new style of expression (like rock 'n' roll) or a problematic social circumstance (like drug abuse). Either way, just as whites were most sure they could ignore events that seemed not to involve them at all, they spread across the nation in a flash. Coming from the bottom of the American social ladder—and for so long rendered untouchable and invisible by slavery and segregation—blacks ironically have been relatively free from the rules enforced by the official culture monitors. . . . Thus it is no surprise that Blacks—who invented such definitely American forms as the spiritual, jazz music and dance, as well as expressions associated with the cultures of rags, blues, bebop, hip hop, and rap—have had such a potent impact on American cultural life and history. What would American culture be without their presence?[27]

Where would America be with respect to trying to continue to implement its ideals if Blacks were out of the picture; or where would it be with respect to trying to bring the lowest of Americans into American rights and opportunities and life, or in providing education for the masses of lowly Americans, or in elevating the public image of people at the lower end of society, if Blacks had not made the kind of contributions they made to these situations. The South did not have a public school system until former Black slaves, after the mid-nineteenth-century war, championed and helped to push this ideal and practicality into southern life.

These comments always make it necessary for Black people to be careful not only about how they use the word or concept of minority and associate it with Blacks, but also how they use the word or concept of invisibilization with respect to them. That word is a reflection of White racist beliefs, thoughts, and perceptions about Black people, where these racists want to relate to Blacks on the basis of their racist fantasies of them, and not on the basis of their actual attributes, relating to Blacks as "Non-Others" as opposed to Others. But a Black presence cannot be invisible in a greater white-people context, not even when that Black presence is segregated. For one thing, Whites never stayed totally out of the segregated Black social world, as southern White trips into that world and White trips into the Black world all over America "after hours," particularly in legendary Harlem of an epochal time, testify.

Black minority status is one of the most fruitful of all Black historical memory sites, and has to be handled with great care. The story of this minority is best told with evidence and facts, not myths. The truth about what Blacks have done in America, not only as a minority but as an enslaved, oppressed, segregated, suppressed, and constantly publicly humiliated and abused minority says more about Blacks and holds more for Black memory than any fictionalized version of this realty can convey.

There is the other thing to consider with respect to Black history and Black memory and projecting them for public view and use. Blacks have lived historically in this country with Whites relating to them on the basis of fantasies about them and lies about them, and with a determination, and certainly a lack of interest, to know anything about them. Blacks are now in a position in their history and life in America, because of the great number of Black intellectuals of all kinds who live here, to have many more outlets for public expression to tell white people "like it is" about Black history and life in this country. Any effort to feed white people myths about Black history and life or Black contributions to American history and the country's internal development will not make a dent in the racist myths that white people still strongly cling to about Black people. These myths will bounce off the racist myths. Even when Whites are not racists they would still look suspiciously if not askance on pronouncements about Black contributions to American history and life, including their lives. They are not accustomed to thinking about Blacks that way any more than other white people are. And they, like the latter, would have the image of Blacks being a minority and all that this registered in their minds about Blacks and what a minority was capable of contributing or not contributing in a country.

The truth about Black people, looked at another way, is also the truth about white people in American history and life. The future of America, in terms of its teleological movement and fulfillment, and also the future of Black people in the teleological movement and fulfillment of their history in the country, is related considerably to white people having a greater truth about Blacks and themselves. This is a greater truth about America that only Black people, using their history as a foundation, can provide. This places a strong responsibility, a strong public responsibility, upon Black historians. They have a responsibility for Black historical memory, but for White and American historical memories as well.

Admittedly, this casts Black historical writing, in this instance, in a political light. But politics is not necessarily detrimental to scholarship. Indeed, political issues or realities have often spawned scholarship, even new areas of scholarship. The quest of scholarship of any kind should be truth, not some absolute, transcendental, unhistorical notion of truth, but truth that a critical analysis of evidence provides. Historical writing, like art, has no sake of its own. Both are produced by people who have the sakes, the motivations, purposes, and intentions to write history and to produce art. If Black historians have the motivation, purpose, and intention of seeking and presenting truth, they will do justice to Black memory sites and Black memories, and they will produce truth and even suggestions of moral postures to guide Black political behavior in America.

Chapter 7

Conclusion

The chapters in this book, as well as other recent writings of mine, represent a long period in my life of wrestling with the subject of history generally and Black history in particular. It has been a process that commenced four decades ago, when I began teaching history in college. There was no Black history then recognizable as such by the history profession and history subculture, although there were Black historians and some white historians who saw something of a distinctive character. The history profession and subculture generally regarded Black history as something approximating "race relations." I never accepted that designation, but I had no clear view of Black history either.

The Black Liberation Struggle of the 1950s and 1960s, the political, social, and physical confrontation between Blacks and Whites, spawned an interest in Black history and helped to contribute to a definition of it, which Black and white historians sought to develop and round out with historical research and writing. The writing on Black chattel slavery in the 1960s and 1970s contributed in a large way to the definition of Black history and its place as a legitimate academic discipline in the history profession and subculture.

However, I had serious reservations about much of the scholarship on Black slavery. In the hands of a number of Black historians it exhibited a strong idyllic and romantic character. I felt that many white historians wrote on slavery less to describe it extensively, analytically, and realistically, than somehow to whitewash the institution and the white slaveholders and other Whites who maintained and perpetuated it. I said as much in a book I published in the late 1970s, entitled *Historians and Slavery*. This was a book that in the first two chapters critiqued the history profession and the history subculture and in the next eight chapters critiqued the writings of several prominent historians on Black slavery in America, such as Carl Degler, Kenneth Stamp, John Blassingame, Eugene Genovese, Stanley Engerman, David Brion-Davis, and William Scarborough. I found a serious lack of concept integrity, many false images, many contradictions and illogical arguments, numerous self-serving statements, and numerous distortions of fact overall in the writings of these historians (and others). It led me to conclude my book in the following manner:

Historically, Black people have been used in this country by white people to serve their interests. That process began over three centuries ago. It continues to this day, taking many forms. One of them is the way historians use the Black historical experience to continue to project the fantasies, illusions, and myths about white people in particular and the continuing American historical process in general. The Black experience not only has to be understood in its full dimensions, but this understanding relates directly to a fuller and more truthful understanding of the larger American historical process. . . . The implications this has for America's future, for the relations between white and non-white, and white and white is enormous. America's future will depend, considerably, upon penetrating and truthful historiographical explanations.[1]

As can be seen, back in the late 1970s I was very optimistic and even idealistic about the impact that historical writing could have on politics or public policy. I do not disavow it altogether, though I am admittedly less sanguine. What I am still very sanguine about, as I was when I wrote *Historians and Slavery*, is critical historical writing. Back in the late 1970s I rejected certain professional and subcultural staples that were declared to produce critical historical writing, things such as "detachment," "disinterested scholarship," "objectivity," "balanced presentation," "minimal use of social science" or "social science theories," and "seeking truth in the middle." I wrote my book *Historians and Slavery* partly to show how easily white historians especially, those who regarded themselves as the rulers of the history profession and subculture and considered themselves the guardians of historical standards and the historical canon, violated all of these things. This was done consciously, but it would seem more often unconsciously. White historians clung tenaciously to many of the myths about white people and America, which were sunk deep in their unconsciousness and played a strong affecting role in their historical research and writing, and particularly, as I saw, in the way they researched and wrote on Black slavery in America. Slaveholders were dictators, denying human dignity, rights, opportunities, and a host of other things that dictators deny people. But not a single one of the white historians I critiqued in *Historians and Slavery* projected that understanding. Stanley Elkins, in his work *Slavery*, argued that southern plantation slavery was oppressive and even produced "Sambos" of the slaves on the plantations. Yet he also argued that the slave masters were "benevolent" in character and behavior. How could benevolent people maintain and perpetuate an oppressive social system and produce psychological deformities by it? The contradiction is glaring, as was the image of slave owners in Degler's, Genovese's, and Engerman's works, which depicted slave masters as essentially agricultural employers. But even John Blassingame projected an image of benevolent slave masters and an idyllic image of the institution in his eagerness to focus on the cultural life of the Black slaves, which he apparently thought could not be discussed adequately, or at all, if the slave masters were depicted as dictatorial and Black chattel slavery as oppressive. Black culture was produced precisely under oppression and exploitation, and whatever mitigation of that oppression and exploitation slaves were able to achieve.

The slave studies, despite the shortcomings of many of them, were able to throw important light on the early life of Black people in the United States. These studies led to other kinds of studies in Black history, and by the 1980s Black history had become a respected and accepted discipline and area of study in the history profession and subculture. But as I argued in the first chapter of this book, there is still considerable confusion as to what constitutes Black history. I tried to resolve that matter in this book. I showed that I was also concerned about the critical focus capacity of Black historical writing, particularly by Black historians. The inadequacy of the critical capacity is reflected in the fact that Black historians still are unable to resolve the question of a Black identity. This is basically a historical evidentiary and cultural and sociological matter. All these approaches make it clear that Black people in America are not Africans and are even different from other black people in the country. Obscuring understanding of this matter is the fact that other black people in this country have been forced to make history with Black people, or to make Black history. But Black history has its own players and subject matter and is not to be confused with the history of other black people in America, or in the Western Hemisphere, or Africa, or Europe, or anywhere else in this world.

The inadequate critical capacity of Black history is reflected in the way Black and black historians, and other kinds of Black or black intellectuals in America, describe Black people by so many different names, and particularly by the different expressions of the African name. It might be argued, as some among these elements do, that the variety of names reduces the "fatigue" or "monotony" of writing and reading Black history. That may well be, but the requirement of the historian is to deal with facts, and critically, and to make interpretations on the basis of critical facts. But the other harm of calling Black people "African Americans," "Afro-Americans," "AfraAmericans," or anything similar is that it projects an image and understanding of Blacks being black Africans, which they are not and have not been for centuries. These are inappropriate names, and inappropriate names, words, concepts, definitions, or images do not make for critical scholarship, including Black historical scholarship.

In the 1970s, when I rejected some of the history profession and subculture's canonical strictures regarding critical historical writing, I felt I had arrived at an understanding of some of the things that would make for critical historical scholarship. I concluded that, generally, it needed a critical analysis that centered in concept integrity, appropriate use of language, and a rigorous use of reasoning logic, which was part of the historical methodology itself. I described this critical analysis in the following manner in *Historians and Slavery*:

A critical analysis of human behavior . . . requires . . . a critical use of reasoning logic. When a historian researches extant evidentiary material, it is necessary to penetrate and apprehend the aspects of reality reflected in the evidence. In written records—which will be our focus here—it is necessary to see if there is a logical and apropos use of words and descriptions. It is necessary to determine if ideas are stated clearly and thoroughly, and that they relate logically to their descriptional and situational contexts. It is necessary to check expressed statements for contradictory thoughts, arguments, or images, or underdeveloped thoughts, arguments or images, or exaggerations of all of these features. It is necessary to determine if the adduced evidence supports the ideas, arguments and images projected from the evidence. The same kind of rigorous use of logic (and this general critical analysis) would be applied to the evaluation of a historians' scholarship on a subject; in short, historiographical essays, monographs or texts.[2]

I used this critical analysis to critique the writing of a number of historians on slavery. The apparatus can be used with other academic disciplines as well, such as sociology, political science, or philosophy. Two of my published books, *Black Intellectuals, Black Cognition, and a Black Aesthetic* and *Racism Matters*, which both mixed history and these other disciplines, made use of this analyses. I employed it in a book published by Praeger, entitled *Black History and Black Identity: A Call for a New Historiography*, which was my effort to trace the origins of the name African and to show in an evidentiary, historical, and cultural way why Black people were not Africans, but were Black people of black African descent; and in which I argued that Black history was just that, and not African or some other kind of history. Another argument of that book was that Black history was not critical enough, and I called for and outlined a new historiography that I thought would make it so.

I used my critical analyses to write the chapters of this book to provide some critical reflections on Black history. A part of my critical analyses that I have not mentioned, but which was employed in *Historians and Slavery*, was my racist analysis. I endeavored to show in Chapter 2 of this book that race and racism were not the same thing, which means that a racial analysis and racist analysis would not be the same things. One is about a biological reality, the other is not about any reality, but some abstract fantasies that are depicted as being representations of embodied or concrete reality. A racist analysis is essential to writing critically on American history and Black history. White, Black, and other historians, and men and women in each group, generally confuse race with racism, with many now denying that race itself exists. This has less to do with the postmodern impact on American historical scholarship than it does with the traditional White behavior of not wanting to deal with racism, and particularly racism's impact on white people and on America's culture and institutions. Many if not most Black historians and other Black or black scholars do not want to deal with racism either, preferring to utilize class and gender analyses or an intersection of the two.

Class and gender concepts and analyses presuppose that the people to which they refer are human beings. A racist analysis shows how people—racists—relate to others as if they were not human beings or full human beings. A racist analysis of American history would take it to a greater depth than a class or gender analysis can take it, or even the two together; the depth of irrationality, perversity, pathology, and immorality, a greater depth that contradicts all discussions in America about liberty, equality, democracy, justice, and freedom. This deeper analysis of American history shows a clear difference between liberty and license, representative government and democratic government, how fanciful the phrase "American innocence" is, and how the phrase "American exception" covers up a multitude of suppressions and degradations in this country's history and social life. A racist analysis does not preclude using other analyses, such as a class or gender analysis, or even a racial analysis. It's necessary to employ and intersect these analyses in various ways. But a racist analysis is not just one among many social analyses, no more important than any of the others. An analysis that shows how people regard and treat other human beings as if they are not human beings or full human beings, or don't even exist, is a very distinct kind of analysis, and is not just another coequal analysis. It is the one to which all the others, certainly in American history and life, have to be connected and predicated upon.

Over the years I added different analyses into my general critical analysis to expand it, always intersecting them with my racist analysis. As I said, I used my critical analysis, even its larger dimension, to write the chapters of this volume. I believe this methodology has helped me to acquire a better understanding of Booker T. Washington and his leadership of Blacks, and his relationship with his essentially northern Black adversaries. It enabled me to extirpate the many erroneous and debilitating images surrounding Booker T. Washington that have been a strong basis, even in historical scholarship, in trying to understand him. This invariably has fostered misunderstanding. Booker T. Washington, as a critical analysis shows (certainly as my critical analysis shows), was a very realistic person, about white people, about Black people, and about what it would take for Blacks to advance in America and the difficulties that they faced trying to do so. The Blacks, as a critical analysis shows, meant southern Blacks, who made up the bulk of the Black population, nine-tenths of that population, during Washington's leadership years. So a historical discussion of Washington has to center on how he thought about, sought to lead, and sought to help southern Blacks, a people "up from slavery," overwhelmingly rural, illiterate, poor, considerably superstitious, functioning from the debilitations of racism/slavery, and now in a very strong and violence racist context. When this context is delineated, one has the critical context in which to evaluate Washington as a person and as the primary or gargantuan leader of Blacks, the efforts he made to try to help Blacks, and also his relationship with Du Bois and his essentially northern Black opposition.

Booker T. Washington has been treated in such a selective manner by white and Black historians, with the selective slant being, consciously and unconsciously, to castigate him. A different kind of selective slant has been used by white historians to write on Abraham Lincoln and to say essentially laudatory things about him, to wrap him up in fanciful, lofty images that seek to hide his negative features: his strong racism, his antidemocratic thinking, his inability, like other white Americans in his day, to distinguish between liberty and license, and the fact that he did not and could not have ended Black chattel slavery in America, because that would take, as it did take, an amendment to the Constitution, which a president—including Abraham Lincoln—could not pass.

History writing is inescapably selective, and thus selectivity with this craft is legitimate. What is not legitimate is to be selective with evidence, analysis, and interpretation to present false images, or to deny, falsify, or suppress realities. This kind of scholarship, historical scholarship that is in flagrant violation of the history canon, has been employed extensively with respect to Booker T. Washington and Abraham Lincoln, but not for the same purposes or for the same benefit. Neither violation has met with much serious criticism, although Lerone Bennett, Jr. has recently voiced strong criticism of the historical selective slanting on Lincoln, including the large role that racism plays in this effort, in his book *Forced into Glory*.[3]

Before the postmodernists and their criticism and rejection of metaphysical or ontological absolutes, and their declaration that history was a form of fiction writing and that "objectivity" was not possible with the discipline, there had been historians who flirted with the idea that historical writing could be a science. This could be done by expanding the historical methodology to add some social science theories and methodologies to it. It was felt that comparative history could contribute to its scientific status. Most historians in America never flirted with this idea. There was especially fear of social science theories, fearing they would destroy historical narratives, promote too much speculation, and be substituted for historical evidence and explanaiton. There were other historians who thought that history was a combination of science and art.

I was never one to believe that history, as an academic area, could be converted into a science. However, I have always felt that history could and has to have a strong scientific capacity. The historical methodology has a scientific orientation (i.e., the rules regarding research, the selection of evidence, the use of evidence, the evidentiary restrictions on interpretation); in short, the history canon, when it is properly observed. My broad critical analysis adds to this scientific capacity. There has always been a failure on the part of most historians to understand something very important about science, which has functioned as a barrier to conceiving history this way, or trying to make it so as much as possible. Historians, as well as others in America, even other academics, think that science is sine qua non with finding "laws" and prediction; that if laws and prediction are not involved in research, modeling, or explanatory efforts, then one is simply not engaged in science.

Physicists, chemists, biologists, or neuroscientists are not always concerned about prediction. They are most often concerned about knowing the components of things they investigate and study, and what the components are made of, how they relate to each other, how they structure, how structures change or develop, and how things are researched and studied function. Neuroscientists seek to map the brain. That involves knowing the general structure and the many parts of the brain, how the parts function, and how the parts relate to each other. This kind of knowledge can be used to try to predict certain kinds of functioning of the brain, or a part or parts of the brain. But gathering the knowledge about the brain has to be as critical, careful, systematic, and judicious as possible; in short, scientifically gathered. Historians gather knowledge too, and when they follow the canon it is done critically, carefully, systematically, and as completely as possible; that is, scientifically, as well. In a very important way, prediction is irrelevant to history, because the past that historians focus on cannot be predicted. The past represents something that has already happened. The task is to try to explain what happened, which requires a methodology with as much scientific capacity as possible. Comparative history could be done with the view of trying to adduce generalizations that can have predictive value. But prediction here cannot be like what occurs in physics or chemistry; that is, cannot be that precise, primarily because human beings can alter any historical or social process of which they are a part, and forecasted knowledge about it can help them do this. Such knowledge could also guide them in vigorously promoting processes to try to implement them. But this would also take decision making, making choices, and engaging in other forms of behavior that might well alter the course pursued, making its outcome problematic or uncertain.

Saying that history should have as large a scientific capacity as it can is also saying that a full scientific capacity is not possible, not because prediction cannot be part of it, but because science simply cannot tell everything there is to know about a human being. There are areas of human beings that are nonmaterial or nonphysical, that are ideational, and that cannot be measured or explained (or adequately explained) by science. Philosophy or art might be able to throw some light on these aspects of human beings. I have for many years felt that history had to embrace philosophy as part of its general methodology to augment its general critical capacity. Art is more problematic for historians, because it knows no restraints and can override or abuse evidence. Thus, art is always something that has to be used with great care by historians as an investigative or analytical tool.

This book shows considerable use of philosophy and social science theories or knowledge, even when I did not employ formal concepts or specify theories, but I like the largest methodological means possible to investigate and to evaluate historical phenomena. This larger methodology makes it possible to get a better grip on concepts and to acquire a better understanding of them and their use. Concepts can be constructed philosophically or sociologically, by social science theories generally. But this is not all that goes into, or should go into, concept construction. History plays a role in that construction as well. Indeed, as I said specifically in Chapter 4, "History . . . plays a very prominent role in determining the authenticity and legitimacy of concepts." History shows, for instance, that "patriarchy" is a reference to men dominating men, not, as is commonly said and believed, men dominating women. History shows that liberalism and conservatism in America are the same things, and that what is today said to be liberalism, so-called modern liberalism, is a combination of liberalism and state socialism. Concepts have to have clear and substantive content, otherwise they will be used in research sloppily, imprecisely, and even in many different ways with many different meanings, which is true of the concepts of racism, liberalism, and democracy, thus producing confusing and inadequate analyses and discussions.

I realize that I am not the typical historian and do not seek to write history in a strict canonical manner. I find the history canon too limiting. I adhere strongly to the canonical obligation of gathering evidence and making interpretations based on evidence, but I feel that my general critical analysis, expanded by philosophy and social science theories, augments my ability to interpret historical evidence and to make historical presentations. I am not a believer in knowledge for knowledge's sake, or truth for truth's sake, but I firmly believe that these are things that historians must pursue and seek to explain.

Notes

CHAPTER 1

1. W. D. Wright, *Black Intellectuals, Black Cognition, and a Black Aesthetic* (Westport, Conn.: Praeger, 1997), 141.

2. Manning Marable, *Beyond Black and White: Transforming African American Politics* (New York: Verso, 1995), 186–187.

3. Barbara J. Fields, "Ideology and Race in American History," in *Region, Race, and Reconstruction: Essays in Honor of C. Vann Woodward*, ed. J. Morgan Kousser and James M. McPherson (New York: Oxford University Press, 1892), 144.

4. Quoted in George Yancy, ed., *African-American Philosophers: 17 Conversations* (New York: Routledge, 1998), 237.

5. Richard A. Goldsby, *Race and Races* (New York: Macmillan, 1971), 5.

6. Sylviane A. Diouf, *Servants of Allah: African Muslims Enslaved in the Americas* (New York: New York University Press, 1998).

7. Ali Mazrui, "On the Concept of 'We are Africans,'" *American Political Science Review* 58, no. 1 (1963): 88–97.

8. Cheikh Anta Diop, *The Cultural Unity of Black Africa: The Domains of Matriarchy and of Patriarchy in Classical Antiquity* (London: Karnak House, 1989).

9. Emmanuel Chukwudi Eze, ed., *African Philosophy: An Anthology* (Malden, Mass.: Blackwell, 1998).

10. Lucius T. Outlaw, Jr., *On Race and Philosophy* (New York: Routledge, 1996), Ch. 4.

11. "Poll Says Blacks Prefer to Be Called Black," *Jet*, 11 February 1991, 8; *Jet*, 30 May 1994, 37; *Jet*, August 1994, 46.

12. Herodotus, *The Histories Revised*, ed. A. R. Burn (New York: Penguin Books, 1972), 283.

13. Quoted in John Henrik Clarke, ed., *New Dimensions in African History: The London Lectures of Dr. Yosef ben-Jochannan and Dr. John Henrik Clarke* (Trenton, N.J.: Africa World Press, 1991), 76–77.

14. Henrico Stephano, ed., *Thesaurus Graecae Linguae*, Vols. 1–2 (Paris: Exudent Ambrosius Firmin Didot, 1831–1856), 2703.

15. Robert H. Hood, *Begrimed and Black: Christian Traditions of Blacks and Blackness* (Minneapolis: Fortress Press, 1994), 25.

16. Bernard Lewis, *Cultures in Conflict: Christians, Muslims, and Jews in the Age of Discovery* (New York: Oxford University Press, 1995), 64–65.

17. Banna to L. Tappan, Westville, 12 March 1841, in John Blassingame, ed., *Slave Testimony: Two Centuries of Letters, Speeches, Interviews, and Autobiographies* (Baton Rouge: Louisiana State University Press, 1977), 38.

18. Abraham Blackford to Mary B. Blackford, Monrovia, 14 February 1846, in ibid., 64.

19. William C. Burke to Mrs. Mary C. Lee, Mount Rest Clay-Ashland, 20 February 1859, in ibid., 103.

20. George Washington Williams, *History of the Negro Race in America from 1619 to 1880*, Vol. 1 (New York: Bergman, 1968), 4.

21. Jacob H. Carruthers, *Intellectual Welfare* (Chicago: Third World Press, 1999).

22. Sterling Stuckey, *Slave Culture: Nationalist Theory and the Foundations of Black America* (New York: Oxford University Press, 1987).

23. Evelyn Brooks Higginbotham, *Righteous Discontent: The Women's Movement in the Black Baptist Church, 1880–1920* (Cambridge: Harvard University Press, 1993).

24. Darlene Clark Hine, *Hine Sight: Black Women and the Reconstruction of American History* (New York: Carlson, 1994).

25. Hazel V. Carby, *Race Men* (Cambridge: Harvard University Press, 1998).

26. Joy James, *Shadow Boxing: Representations of Black Feminist Politics* (New York: St. Martin's Press, 1999).

27. Stuckey, *Slave Culture.*

28. Joseph E. Holloway, "Introduction," in *Africanisms in American Culture*, ed. Joseph E. Holloway (Bloomington: Indiana University Press, 1990), xx.

29. Ibid.

30. William Edward Burghardt Du Bois, *The Souls of Black Folk* (Millwood, N.Y.: Kraus-Thompson, 1973).

31. "Poll Says Blacks Prefer to Be Called Black," 8.

32. *Jet*, 30 May 1994, 37.

33. M. Itua, "Africans Do Not Want to Be Africans," in *The Black Think Tank*, ed. Naiwu Osahon (Lagos: International Coordinating Committee of the 7th Pan African Congress, 1992), 4.

34. Robert L. Harris, Jr., "Coming of Age: The Transformation of Afro-American Historiography," *The Journal of Negro History* 67, no. 2 (1982): 118.

35. Ibid., 116.

36. Paul Gilroy, *The Black Atlantic Modernity and Double Consciousness* (Cambridge: Harvard University Press, 1993).

CHAPTER 2

1. Lloyd A. Thompson, *Romans and Blacks* (Norman: University of Oklahoma Press, 1989), 10.

2. Ibid., 2.

3. Ibid., 18.

4. W.E.B. Du Bois, *The Negro* (New York: Oxford University Press, 1970), 9.

5. L. C. Dunn, "Race and Biology," in *Race, Science and Society*, ed. Leo Kuper (New York: Columbia University Press, 1975), 11–12.

6. George M. Frederickson, *The Arrogance of Race: Historical Perspectives on Slavery, Racism, and Social Inequality* (Middletown, Conn.: Wesleyan University Press, 1988), 189.

7. W.E.B. Du Bois, *The Autobiography of W.E.B. Du Bois: A Soliloquy on Viewing My Life from the Last Decade of Its First Century* (New York: International, 1968).

8. W.E.B. Du Bois, "Disfranchisement," in *W.E.B. Du Bois Speaks: Speeches and Addresses 1890–1919*, ed. Philip S. Foner (New York: Pathfinder Press, 1970), 235.

9. W.E.B. Du Bois to Elizabeth Prophet, 20 November 1934, in *The Correspondence of W. E. B. Du Bois*, Vol. 2, *Selections, 1934–1944*, ed. Herbert Aptheker (Amherst: University of Massachusetts Press, 1976), 40.

10. W.E.B. Du Bois, "The Negro and the Warsaw Ghetto," in *W.E.B. Du Bois Speaks: Speeches and Addresses, 1920–1963*, ed. Philip S. Foner (New York: Pathfinder Press, 1970), 259.

11. W.E.B. Du Bois, "Prospect of a World Without Racial Conflict," in ibid., 124.

12. W. D. Wright, "The Faces of Racism," *Western Journal of Black Studies* 11, no. 4 (1987): 168–176.

13. W. D. Wright, *Racism Matters* (Westport, Conn.: Praeger, 1998).

14. Nancy Tuana, *Woman and the History of Philosophy* (New York: Paragon Press, 1992), xiv.

15. Saul Dubow, *Scientific Racism in Modern South Africa* (Cambridge: Cambridge University Press, 1995), 25–26.

16. Quoted in Anthony T. Browder, *Nile Valley Contributions to Civilization: Exploding the Myths*, Vol. 1 (Washington, D.C.: Institute of Karmic Guidance, 1992), 17.

17. Quoted in Garett Ward Sheldon, *The Political Philosophy of Thomas Jefferson* (Baltimore: Johns Hopkins University Press, 1991), 130.

18. Quoted in Jan Nederveen Pieterse, *White on Black: Images of Africa and Blacks in Western Popular Culture* (New Haven, Conn.: Yale University Press, 1992), 34.

19. Quoted in St. Clair Drake, *Black Folk Here and There: An Essay in History and Anthropology*, Vol. 1 (Los Angeles: Center for Afro-American Studies, University of California at Los Angeles, 1987), 27.

20. Quoted in Pieterse, *White on Black*, 42.

21. Quoted in Will Durant and Ariel Durant, *The Lessons of History* (New York: MJF Books, 1968), 25.

22. William H. Tucker, *The Science and Politics of Racial Research* (Urbana: University of Illinois Press, 1994), 10–11.

23. W. D. Wright, *Black Intellectuals, Black Cognition, and a Black Aesthetic* (Westport, Conn.: Praeger, 1997), 135.

24. Kwame Anthony Appiah, *In My Father's House: Africa in the Philosophy of Culture* (New York: Oxford University Press, 1992).

25. Cornel West, *Race Matters* (Boston: Beacon Press, 1993).

26. Frederick Douglass, "Prejudice Against Color," in *The Life and Writings of Frederick Douglass*, Vol. 2, *Pre–Civil War Decade 1850–1860*, ed. Philip S. Foner (New York: International, 1950), 129.

27. There were Enlightenment thinkers who opposed slavery, such as Thomas Hobbes and Jean Jacques Rousseau, but both men and others like them were white supremacists/ebonicists and believed that black people were "innately" "inferior" to white people.

28. Nathan I. Huggins, *Black Odyssey: The African-American Ordeal in Slavery* (New York: Random House, 1990), xvi.

29. John Blassingame, *The Slave Community: Plantation Life in the Antebellum South* (New York: Oxford University Press, 1972).

30. Laurence Shore, "The Poverty of Tragedy in Historical Writing on Southern Slavery," *The South Atlantic Quarterly* 85, no. 2 (1986): 147–148.

CHAPTER 3

1. William Henry Ferris to Booker T. Washington, 26 November 1907, in *The Booker T. Washington Papers*, Vol. 9, *1906–08*, ed. Louis R. Harlan, Raymond Smock, and Nan E. Woodruff (Urbana: University of Illinois Press, 1980), 410.

2. Booker T. Washington, "An Address before the National Negro Business League in Chicago," in *The Booker T. Washington Papers*, Vol. 2, *1860–89*, ed. Louis R. Harlan, Pete Daniel, Raymond W. Smock, and William M. Welty (Urbana: University of Illinois Press, 1972), 584.

3. W.E.B. Du Bois, "On Segregation," in *A W.E.B. Du Bois Reader*, ed. Andrew G. Paschal (New York: Collier Books, 1971), 134.

4. W.E.B. Du Bois, *The Crisis* 14, no. 5 (1934): 147.

5. Booker T. Washington, "An Address before the Afro-American Council," in *The Booker T. Washington Papers*, Vol. 7, *1903–4*, ed. Louis R. Harlan and Raymond Smock (Urbana: University of Illinois Press, 1977), 191.

6. David Levering Lewis, *W.E.B. Du Bois: Biography of a Race 1868–1919* (New York: Henry Holt, 1993), 308.

7. Quoted in ibid., 311.

8. James Weldon Johnson, *Along This Way: The Autobiography of James Weldon Johnson* (New York: Viking Press, 1933), 203–204.

9. Quoted in Robert L. Factor, *The Black Response to America: Men, Ideals, and Organization from Frederick Douglass to the NAACP* (Reading, Mass.: Addison-Wesley, 1970), 233.

10. John Brown Childs, *Leadership, Conflict, and Cooperation in Afro-American Social Thought* (Philadelphia: Temple University Press, 1989).

11. Robert Michael Franklin, *Liberating Visions: Human Fulfillment and Social Justice in African-American Thought* (Minneapolis: Fortress Press, 1990).

12. Louis R. Harlan, *Booker T. Washington: The Wizard of Tuskegee 1901–1915* (New York: Oxford University Press, 1983), viii.

13. Quoted in W. D. Wright, "The Thought and Leadership of Kelly Miller," *Phylon* 39, no. 2 (1978): 181.

14. W.E.B. Du Bois, *The Souls of Black Folk* (Millwood, N.Y.: Kraus-Thompson, 1973), 49.

15. W.E.B. Du Bois, *Dusk of Dawn: An Essay Toward an Autobiography of a Race Concept* (New York: Schocken Books, 1968), 72.

16. W.E.B. Du Bois, *The Autobiography of W.E.B. Du Bois: A Soliloquy on Viewing My Life from the Last Decade of Its First Century* (New York: International, 1968), 246–247.

17. Ibid., 70.

18. Ibid., 241.

19. Johnson, *Along This Way*, 313.

20. August Meier, *Negro Thought in America, 1880–1915: Racial Ideologies in the Age of Booker T. Washington* (Ann Arbor: University of Michigan Press, 1963), 245.

21. Nell Irvin Painter, *Standing at Armageddon: The United States, 1877–1919* (New York: W. W. Norton, 1987), 223.

22. Quoted in Larry Cuban, "A Strategy for Racial Peace: Negro Leadership in Cleveland, 1900–1919," *Phylon* 28, no. 3 (1967): 308.

23. "An Account of Washington's Reception in New England," in *The Booker T. Washington Papers*, Vol. 10, *1909–11*, ed. Louis R. Harlan, Raymond Smock, Geraldine McTigue, and Nan E. Woodruff (Urbana: University of Illinois Press, 1981), 411–412.

24. William Anthony Avery, "An Account of Washington's Louisiana Tour," in *The Booker T. Washington Papers*, Vol. 13, *1914–1915*, ed. Louis R. Harlan, Raymond Smock, Susan Valenza, and Sade M. Harlan (Urbana: University of Illinois Press, 1984), 322–323.

25. Mary White Ovington to W.E.B. Du Bois, 11 April 1914, in *The Correspondence of W.E.B. Du Bois*, Vol. 1, *Selections, 1877–1934*, ed. Herbert Aptheker (Amherst: University of Massachusetts Press, 1973), 192.

26. J. E. Spingarn to W.E.B. Du Bois, 24 October 1914, in ibid., 202.

27. Charles Flint Kellogg, *NAACP: A History of the National Association for the Advancement of Colored People* (Baltimore: Johns Hopkins University Press, 1967), 130.

28. Quoted in B. Joyce Ross, *J. E. Spingarn and the Rise of the NAACP* (New York: Atheneum, 1972), 25.

29. Eugene Levy, *James Weldon Johnson: Black Leader, Black Voice* (Chicago: University of Chicago Press, 1973), 172.

30. John T. McCartney, *Black Power Ideologies: An Essay in African-American Political Thought* (Philadelphia: Temple University Press, 1992), 65–66.

31. Mary White Ovington, *Black and White Sat Down Together: The Reminiscences of an NAACP Founder*, ed. Ralph E. Luker (New York: Feminist Press at the City University of New York, 1995), 58.

32. Booker T. Washington to Emmett Jay Scott, 16 January 1914, in *The Booker T. Washington Papers*, Vol. 12, *1912–14*, ed. Louis R. Harlan and Raymond Smock (Urbana: University of Illinois Press, 1982), 417.

33. Booker T. Washington to Timothy Thomas Fortune, 28 January 1914, in ibid., 420.

34. Du Bois, *Dusk of Dawn*, 95.

35. Du Bois, *Autobiography*, 259.

36. Harlan, *Booker T. Washington: The Wizard*, 323.

37. Ibid., ix.

38. Booker T. Washington to Theodore Roosevelt, 29 July 1904, in *The Booker T. Washington Papers*, Vol. 8, *1904–06*, ed. Louis R. Harlan, Raymond Smock, and Geraldine McTigue (Urbana: University of Illinois Press, 1979), 34.

39. Booker T. Washington to William Howard Taft, 21 October 1909, in *Washington Papers*, vol. 10, 184–185.

40. Booker T. Washington to William Henry Baldwin, Jr., 11 September 1903, in *Washington Papers*, no. 7, 282.

41. Booker T. Washington to William Goodell Frost, 11 February 1903, in ibid., 68.

42. Vaclav Havel, *The Art of the Impossible: Politics as Morality in Practice* (New York: Knopf, 1997), 84.

43. Louis R. Harlan, "Booker T. Washington in Biographical Perspective," in *Booker T. Washington in Perspective: Essays of Louis R. Harlan*, ed. Raymond Smock (Jackson: University Press of Mississippi, 1988), 21.

44. Louis R. Harlan, *Booker T. Washington: The Making of a Black Leader 1856–1901* (New York: Oxford University Press, 1972), viii.

45. Quoted in Harlan, *Booker T. Washington: The Wizard*, x.

46. Du Bois, *The Souls of Black Folk*, 43.

47. Factor, *The Black Response*, 187.

48. Harlan, *Booker T. Washington: The Wizard*, viii.

49. Manning Marable, "Booker T. Washington and the Political Economy of Black Education in the United States 1880–1915," in *A Different Vision: African American Economic Thought*, Vol. 1, ed. Thomas D. Boston (New York: Routledge, 1997), 169.

50. Thomas C. Holt, "The Political Uses of Alienation: W.E.B. Du Bois on Politics, Race, and Culture, 1903–1940," *American Quarterly* 42, no. 2 (1990): 315.

51. W.E.B. Du Bois to Booker T. Washington, Wilberforce, 24 September 1895, in *The Correspondence of W.E.B. Du Bois*, vol. 1, 39.

52. Booker T. Washington, "A Sunday Evening Talk: Self Denial," in *The Booker T. Washington Papers*, Vol. 3, *1889–95*, ed. Louis R. Harlan, Stuart B. Kaufman, and Raymond Smock (Urbana: University of Illinois Press, 1974), 131.

53. Booker T. Washington, "A Sunday Evening Talk: The Work to Be Done by Tuskegee Graduates," in ibid., 551.

54. Booker T. Washington, *Character Building* (New York: Doubleday, Page, 1902), 40–41.

55. Quoted in *The Southern Letter* 4, no. 9 (1898): 1.

56. Quoted in ibid., 3.

57. Quoted in *The Southern Letter*, 7, no. 10 (1890): 1.

58. Quoted in *The Southern Letter*, 13, no. 11 (1896): 3.

59. Quoted in *The Southern Letter*, 17, no. 4 (1901): 3.

60. Earl W. Crosby, "The Roots of Black Agricultural Extension Work," *The Historian* 39, no. 2 (1977): 228–247.

61. Du Bois, *Autobiography*, 239.

62. Harlan, *Booker T. Washington: The Making*, ix.

63. Du Bois, *Autobiography*, 239.

64. Thomas Dixon, Jr., "Booker T. Washington and the Negro," in *The Poisoned Tongue: A Documentary History of American Racism and Prejudice*, ed. Stanley Feldstein (New York: William Morrow, 1972), 203 (italics original).

CHAPTER 4

1. Thomas C. Holt, "Introduction: Whither Now and Why?" in *The State of Afro-American History: Past, Present, and Future*, ed. Darlene Clark Hine (Baton Rouge: Louisiana State University Press, 1986), 5.

2. John Hope Franklin, "The New Negro History," *Journal of Negro History* 43, no. 2 (1957): 95–97.

3. Vincent Harding, "Beyond Chaos: Black History and the Search for the New Land," in *Amistad I*, ed. John A. Williams and Charles F. Harris (New York: Vintage Books, 1970), 267–292.

4. Benjamin Quarles, "Black History Unbound," *Daedalus* 103, no. 2 (1974): 165–166.

5. Nathan I. Huggins, "Integrating Afro-American History into American History," in Hine, *The State of Afro-American History*, 157.

6. Nathan I. Huggins, "Afro-American History: Myths, Heroes, Reality," in *Key Issues in the Afro-American Experience, Vol. 1, to 1877*, ed. Nathan I. Huggins, Martin Kilson, and Daniel Fox (New York: Harcourt Brace Jovanovich, 1971), 5.

7. Huggins, "Integrating Afro-American History," 166–167.

8. Ibid., 167.

9. Nell Irvin Painter, "Bias and Synthesis in History," *Journal of American History* 74, no. 1 (1987): 110.

10. Nell Irvin Painter, *Standing at Armageddon: The United States, 1877–1919* (New York: W. W. Norton, 1987), 230.

11. Darlene Clark Hine, *Hine Sight: Black Women and the Reconstruction of American History* (New York: Carlson, 1994), 53.

12. Nell Irvin Painter, "Comment," in Hine, *The State of Afro-American History*, 81–82.

13. Hine, *Hine Sight*, xvii.

14. Ibid., xvii–xviii.

15. Ibid., 51–52.

16. Ibid., 52.

17. Ibid.

18. Painter, "Comment," 81.

19. bell hooks, *Ain't I a Woman: Black Women and Feminism* (Boston: South End Press, 1981), 1.

20. bell hooks, *Yearning: Race, Gender, and Cultural Politics* (Boston: South End Press, 1990).

21. Patricia Hill Collins, *Fighting Words: Black Women and the Search for Justice* (Minneapolis: University of Minnesota Press, 1998), 50.

22. Quoted in W. D. Wright, "The Faces of Racism," *Western Journal of Black Studies* 11, no. 4 (1987): 173.

23. Barbara Hilkert Andolsen, *"Daughters of Jefferson, Daughters of BootBlacks"* (Macon, Ga.: Mercer University Press, 1986), x.

24. Quoted in Collins, *Fighting Words*, 132.

25. William Julius Wilson, *The Declining Significance of Race: Blacks and Changing American Institutions*, 2d ed. (Chicago: University of Chicago Press, 1980).

26. Quoted in Joy James, *Shadow Boxing: Representations of Black Feminist Politics* (New York: St. Martin's Press, 1999), 155.

27. Quoted in ibid., 164–165.

28. Gail Elizabeth Wyatt, *Stolen Woman: Reclaiming Our Sexuality, Taking Back Our Lives* (New York: John Wiley & Sons, 1997), xvii.

29. W.E.B. Du Bois, *The Crisis* 23, no. 5 (1922): 199.

30. hooks, *Yearning*, 16.

31. Michele Wallace, *Black Macho and the Myth of the Superwoman* (New York: Warner Books, 1979).

32. Shirley J. Yee, *Black Women Abolitionists: A Study in Activism, 1828–1860* (Knoxville: University of Tennessee Press, 1992).

33. Paula Giddings, *When and Where I Enter: The Impact of Black Women on Race and Sex in America* (New York: William Morrow, 1984).

34. Lawrence J. Friedman, *Inventors of the Promised Land* (New York: Alfred A. Knopf, 1975).

35. C. Vann Woodward, "Clio with Soul," *Journal of American History* 16, no. 1 (1969): 18.

CHAPTER 5

1. Cf. Bruce Mazlish, "Comparing Global History to World History," *Journal of Interdisciplinary History* 28, no. 3 (1998): 385–395.

2. W.E.B. Du Bois, "The Souls of White Folk," in *W.E.B. Du Bois: A Reader*, ed. Meyer Weinberg (New York: Harper & Row, 1970), 303.

3. Booker T. Washington, "The Negro and the Signs of Civilization," in *The Booker T. Washington Papers*, Vol. 6, *1901–02*, ed. Louis R. Harlan, Raymond Smock, and Barbara S. Kraft (Urbana: University of Illinois Press, 1977). 300.

4. Ibid.

5. Gunnar Myrdal, *An American Dilemma: The Negro Problem and Modern Democracy* (New York: Harper & Row, 1994).

6. Booker T. Washington, *Up from Slavery* (New York: Oxford University Press, 1995), 3.

7. Jacob H. Carruthers, *Intellectual Warfare* (Chicago: Third World Press, 1999), xxv.

8. Vernon J. Dixon and Badi G. Foster, eds., *Beyond Black and White: An Alternative America* (Boston: Beacon Press, 1971).

9. W.E.B. Du Bois, *The Souls of Black Folk* (Millwood, N.Y.: Kraus-Thompson, 1973), 4.

10. W.E.B. Du Bois, "Whither Now and Why," in *The Education of Black People: Ten Critiques 1906–1960 by W.E.B. Du Bois*, ed. Herbert Aptheker (Amherst: University of Massachusetts Press, 1973), 150.

11. E. Franklin Frazier, "The Failure of the Negro Intellectual," in *E. Franklin Frazier on Race Relations: Selected Writings*, ed. G. Franklin Edwards (Chicago: University of Chicago Press, 1968), 268.

12. Bernard R. Boxill, *Blacks and Social Justice*, rev. ed. (Lanham, Md.: Rowman and Liddlefield, 1992).

13. W. D. Wright, *Black Intellectuals, Black Cognition, and a Black Aesthetic* (Westport, Conn.: Praeger, 1997), 66.

14. Quoted in ibid., 68–69.

15. Quoted in Julius Lester, *To Be a Slave* (New York: Dell, 1968), 88.

16. Quoted in Norman P. Yetman, ed., *Life under the "Peculiar Institution": Selections from the Slave Narrative Collection* (New York: Holt, Rinehart and Winston, 1970), 45.

17. Quoted in ibid., 217.

18. Quoted in ibid., 192.

19. Boxill, *Blacks and Social Justice*, 173.

20. Wright, *Black Intellectuals*, 74.

21. Du Bois, *The Souls of Black Folk*, 4.

22. Hazel V. Corby, *Race Men* (Cambridge: Harvard University Press, 1998).

CHAPTER 6

1. Genevieve Fabre and Robert O'Meally, eds., *History and Memory in African-American Culture* (New York: Oxford University Press, 1994), 7.

2. Ibid., 6.

3. Alan Wildman, "Who Writes Our Scripts?" *Russian Review* 55, no. 2 (1996): vi.

4. Keith Windschuttle, *The Killing of History: How Literary Critics and Social Theorists Are Murdering Our Past* (New York: Free Press, 1996), 2.

5. Michel-Rolph Trouillot, *Silencing the Past: Power and the Production of History* (Boston: Beacon Press, 1995), 6.

6. Thomas A. Bailey, "The Mythmakers of American History," *Journal of American History* 55, no. 1 (1968): 7–8.

7. Louis R. Harlan, "Broadening the Concept of History," *Journal of Southern History* 57, no. 1 (1991): 5.

8. W.E.B. Du Bois, *Black Reconstruction in America: An Essay Toward a History of the Part Which Black Folk Played in the Attempt to Reconstruct Democracy in America, 1860–1880* (New York: Simon & Schuster, 1992), 727.

9. Trouillot, *Silencing the Past*, 26.

10. Langston Hughes, "The Negro Artist and the Racial Mountain," in *The Black Aesthetic*, ed. Addison Gayle, Jr. (Garden City, N.Y.: Doubleday, 1972), 172.

11. Toni Morrison, "The Site of Memory," in *Inventing Truth: The Art and Craft of Memoir*, ed. William Zinsser (New York: Book-of-the-Month Club, 1987), 112.

12. Quoted in Philip S. Foner, ed., *The Life and Writings of Frederick Douglass*, Vol. 2, *Pre–Civil War Decade, 1850–1860* (New York: International, 1950), 192.

13. Morrison, "The Site of Memory," 110–111.

14. Stanley Elkins, *Slavery: A Problem in American Institutional and Intellectual Life* (New York: Grosset & Dunlap, 1963).

15. Benjamin Quarles, *Lincoln and the Negro* (New York: Oxford University Press, 1962), 36.

16. John Hope Franklin, *Racial Equality in America* (Chicago: University of Chicago Press, 1976), 58.

17. Quoted in Philip S. Foner, ed., *The Life and Writings of Frederick Douglass*, Vol. 4, *Reconstruction and After* (New York: International, 1955), 312.

18. David Herbert Donald, *Lincoln* (New York: Simon & Schuster, 1995), 167.

19. Nathan Huggins, "Integrating Afro-American History into American History," in *The State of Afro-American History: Past, Present, and Future*, ed. Darlene Clark Hine (Baton Rouge: Louisiana State University Press, 1986), 164.

20. Ibid.

21. Jane Campbell, *Mythic Black Fiction: The Transformation of History* (Knoxville: University of Tennessee Press, 1986), ix.

22. Madhu Dubey, *Black Women Novelists and the Nationalist Aesthetic* (Bloomington: Indiana University Press, 1994).

23. Deborah Gray White, *Too Heavy a Load: Black Women in Defense of Themselves 1894–1994* (New York: W. W. Norton, 1999).

24. Toni Morrison, *Playing in the Dark: Whiteness and the Literacy Imagination* (Cambridge: Harvard University Press, 1992).

25. Mechal Sobel, *The World They Made Together: Black and White Values in Eighteenth Century Virginia* (Princeton, N.J.: Princeton University Press, 1987); William D. Piersen, *Black Legacy: America's Hidden Heritage* (Amherst: University of Massachusetts Press, 1993).

26. Quoted in Fabre and O'Meally, *History and Memory in African-American Culture*, 4.

27. Ibid., 4–5.

CONCLUSION

1. W. D. Wright, *Historians and Slavery: A Critical Analysis of Perspectives and Irony in American Slavery and Other Recent Works* (Washington, D.C.: University Press of America, 1978), 310–311.

2. Ibid., 19.

3. Lerone Bennett, Jr., *Forced into Glory: Abraham Lincoln's White Dream* (Chicago: Johnson, 2000).

Selected Bibliography

Andolsen, Barbara Hilkert. *"Daughters of Jefferson, Daughters of Boot-Blacks."* Macon, Ga.: Mercer University Press, 1986.

Appiah, Kwame Anthony. *In My Father's House: Africa in the Philosophy of Culture.* New York: Oxford University Press, 1992.

Aptheker, Herbert, ed. *The Autobiography of W.E.B. Du Bois: A Soliloquy on Viewing My Life from the Last Decade of Its First Century.* New York: International, 1968.

Aptheker, Herbert, ed. *The Correspondence of W.E.B. Du Bois.* Vol. 1, *Selections, 1877–1934.* Amherst: University of Massachusetts Press, 1973.

Blassingame, John. *The Slave Community: Plantation Life in the Antebellum South.* New York: Oxford University Press, 1972.

Blassingame, John, ed. *Slave Testimony: Two Centuries of Letters, Speeches, Interviews, and Autobiographies.* Baton Rouge: Louisiana State University Press, 1977.

Boxill, Bernard R. *Blacks and Social Justice.* Rev. ed. Lanham, Md.: Rowman and Littlefield, 1992.

Browder, Anthony T. *Nile Valley Contributions to Civilization: Exploding the Myths.* Vol. 1. Washington, D.C.: Institute of Karmic Guidance, 1992.

Campbell, Jane. *Mythic Black Fiction: The Transformation of History.* Knoxville: University of Tennessee Press, 1986.

Carby, Hazel V. *Race Men*. Cambridge: Harvard University Press, 1998.

Carruthers, Jacob H. *Intellectual Welfare*. Chicago: Third World Press, 1999.

Childs, John Brown. *Leadership, Conflict, and Cooperation in Afro-American Social Thought*. Philadelphia: Temple University Press, 1989.

Clarke, John Henrik, ed. *New Dimensions in African History: The London Lectures of Dr. Yosef ben-Jochannan and Dr. John Henrik Clarke*. Trenton, N.J.: Africa World Press, 1991.

Collins, Patricia Hill. *Fighting Words: Black Women and the Search for Justice*. Minneapolis: University of Minnesota Press, 1998.

Diop, Cheikh Anta. *The Cultural Unity of Black Africa: The Domains of Matriarchy and of Patriarchy in Classical Antiquity*. London: Karnak House, 1989.

Diouf, Sylviane A. *Servants of Allah: Africa Muslims Enslaved in the Americas*. New York: New York University Press, 1998.

Dixon, Thomas, Jr. "Booker T. Washington and the Negro." In *The Poisoned Tongue: A Documentary History of American Racism and Prejudice*, edited by Stanley Feldstein. New York: William Morrow, 1972.

Drake, St. Clair. *Black Folk Here and There: An Essay in History and Anthropology*. Vol. 1. Los Angeles: Center for Afro-American Studies, University of California at Los Angeles, 1987.

Dubey, Madhu. *Black Women Novelists and the Nationalist Aesthetic*. Bloomington: Indiana University Press, 1994.

Du Bois, W.E.B. *Black Reconstruction in America: An Essay Toward a History of the Part Which Black Folk Played in the Attempt to Reconstruct Democracy in America, 1860–1880*. New York: Simon & Schuster, 1992.

Du Bois, W.E.B. *Dusk of Dawn: An Essay toward an Autobiography of a Race Concept*. New York: Schocken Books, 1968.

Du Bois, W.E.B. *The Negro*. New York: Oxford University Press, 1970.

Du Bois, W.E.B. *The Souls of Black Folk*. Millwood, N.Y.: Kraus-Thompson, 1973.

Du Bois, W.E.B. "Whither Now and Why." In *The Education of Black People: Ten Critiques 1906–1960*, edited by Herbert Aptheker. Amherst: University of Massachusetts Press, 1973.

Dubow, Saul. *Scientific Racism in Modern South Africa*. Cambridge: Cambridge University Press, 1995.

Eze, Emmanuel Chukwudi, ed. *African Philosophy: An Anthology*. Malden, Mass.: Blackwell, 1998.

Fabre, Genevieve, and Robert O'Meally, eds. *History and Memory in African-American Culture*. New York: Oxford University Press, 1994.

Factor, Robert L. *The Black Response to America: Men, Ideals, and Organization from Frederick Douglass to the NAACP*. Reading, Mass.: Addison-Wesley, 1970.

Fields, Barbara J. "Ideology and Race in American History." In *Region, Race and Reconstruction: Essays in Honor of C. Vann Woodward*, edited by Morgan Kousser and James M. McPherson. New York: Oxford University Press, 1982.

Foner, Philip S., ed. *W.E.B. Du Bois Speaks: Speeches and Addresses 1890–1919*. New York: Pathfinder Press, 1970.

Foner, Philip S., ed. *W.E.B. Du Bois Speaks: Speeches and Addresses 1920–1963*. New York: Pathfinder Press, 1970.

Franklin, John Hope. *Racial Equality in America*. Chicago: University of Chicago Press, 1976.

Franklin, Robert Michael. *Liberating Visions: Human Fulfillment and Social Justice in African-American Thought*. Minneapolis: Fortress Press, 1990.

Frazier, E. Franklin. "The Failure of the Negro Intellectual." In *E. Franklin Frazier on Race Relations: Selected Writings*, edited by G. Franklin Edwards. Chicago: University of Chicago Press, 1968.

Frederickson, George M. *The Arrogance of Race: Historical Perspectives on Slavery, Racism, and Social Inequality*. Middletown, Conn.: Wesleyan University Press, 1988.

Friedman, Lawrence J. *Inventors of the Promised Land*. New York: Alfred A. Knopf, 1975.

Giddings, Paula. *When and Where I Enter: The Impact of Black Women on Race and Sex in America*. New York: William Morrow, 1984.

Gilroy, Paul. *The Black Atlantic Modernity and Double Consciousness*. Cambridge: Harvard University Press, 1993.

Goldsby, Richard A. *Race and Races*. New York: Macmillan, 1971.

Harding, Vincent. "Beyond Chaos: Black History and the Search for the New Land." In *Amistad I*, edited by John A. Williams and Charles F. Harris. New York: Vintage Books, 1970.

Harlan, Louis R. "Booker T. Washington in Biographical Perspective." In *Booker T. Washington in Perspective: Essays of Louis R. Harlan*, edited by Raymond Smock. Jackson: University Press of Mississippi, 1988.

Harlan, Louis R. *Booker T. Washington: The Wizard of Tuskegee 1901–1915*. New York: Oxford University Press, 1983.

Harlan, Louis R., and Raymond Smock, eds. *The Booker T. Washington Papers*. Vol. 12, *1912–14*. Urbana: University of Illinois Press, 1982.

Harlan, Louis R., Raymond Smock, and Geraldine McTigue, eds. *The Booker T. Washington Papers*. Vol. 8, *1904–06*. Urbana: University of Illinois Press, 1979.

Harlan, Louis R., Raymond Smock, and Nan E. Woodruff, eds. *The Booker T. Washington Papers*. Vol. 9, *1906–08*. Urbana: University of Illinois Press, 1980.

Havel, Vaclav. *The Art of the Impossible: Politics as Morality in Practice*. New York: Knopf, 1997.

Herodotus. *The Histories Revised*. Edited by A. R. Burn. New York: Penguin Books, 1972.

Higginbotham, Evelyn Brooks. *Righteous Discontent: The Women's Movement in the Black Baptist Church, 1880–1920*. Cambridge: Harvard University Press, 1993.

Hine, Darlene Clark. *Hine Sight: Black Women and the Reconstruction of American History*. New York: Carlson, 1994.

Holloway, Joseph E., ed. *Africanisms in American Culture*. Bloomington: Indiana University Press, 1990.

Holt, Thomas C. "Introduction: Whither Now and Why?" In *The State of Afro-American History Past, Present, and Future*, edited by Darlene Clark Hine. Baton Rouge: Louisiana State University Press, 1986.

hooks, bell. *Ain't I a Woman: Black Women and Feminism*. Boston: South End Press, 1981.

Huggins, Nathan I. "Afro-American History: Myths, Heroes, Reality." In *Key Issues in the Afro-American Experience*. Vol. 1, *to 1877*, edited by Nathan I. Huggins, Martin Kilson, and Daniel Fox. New York: Harcourt Brace Jovanovich, 1971.

Huggins, Nathan I. *Black Odyssey: The African-American Ordeal in Slavery*. New York: Random House, 1990.

Hughes, Langston. "The Negro Artist and the Racial Mountain." In *The Black Aesthetic*, edited by Addison Gayle, Jr. Garden City, N.Y.: Doubleday, 1972.

Itua, M. "Africans Do Not Want to Be Africans." In *The Black Think Tank*, edited by Naiwu Osahon. Lago: International Coordinating Committee of the 7th Pan African Congress, 1992.

James, Joy. *Shadow Boxing: Representations of Black Feminist Politics*. New York: St. Martin's Press, 1999.

Johnson, James Weldon. *Along This Way: The Autobiography of James Weldon Johnson*. New York: Viking Press, 1933.

Kellogg, Charles Flint. *NAACP: A History of the National Association for the Advancement of Colored People*. Baltimore: Johns Hopkins University Press, 1967.

Levering Lewis, David. *W.E.B. Du Bois: Biography of a Race 1868–1919*. New York: Henry Holt, 1993.

Levy, Eugene. *James Weldon Johnson: Black Leader, Black Voice*. Chicago: University of Chicago Press, 1973.

Lewis, Bernard. *Cultures in Conflict: Christians, Muslims, and Jews in the Age of Discovery*. New York: Oxford University Press, 1995.

Marable, Manning. *Beyond Black and White: Transforming African American Politics*. New York: Verso, 1995.

Mazlish, Bruce. "Comparing Global History to World History." *Journal of Interdisciplinary History* 28 (1998): 285–395.

McCartney, John T. *Black Power Ideologies: An Essay in African-American Political Thought*. Philadelphia: Temple University Press, 1992.

Meier, August. *Negro Thought in America, 1880–1915: Racial Ideologies in the Age of Booker T. Washington*. Ann Arbor: University of Michigan Press, 1963.

Morrison, Toni. "The Site of Memory." In *Inventing Truth: The Art and Craft of Memoir*, edited by William Zinsser. New York: Book-of-the-Month Club, 1987.

Myrdal, Gunnar. *An American Dilemma: The Negro Problem and Modern Democracy*. New York: Harper & Row, 1994.

Outlaw, Lucius T., Jr. *On Race and Philosophy*. New York: Routledge, 1996.

Ovington, Mary White. *Black and White Sat Down Together: The Reminiscences of an NAACP Founder.* Edited by Ralph E. Luker. New York: Feminist Press at the City University of New York, 1995.

Painter, Nell Irvin. *Standing at Armageddon: The United States, 1877–1919.* New York: W. W. Norton, 1987.

Pieterse, Jan Nederveen. *White on Black: Images of Africa and Blacks in Western Popular Culture.* New Haven, Conn.: Yale University Press, 1992.

Quarles, Benjamin. *Lincoln and the Negro.* New York: Oxford University Press, 1962.

Ross, Joyce B. *J. E. Spingarn and the Rise of the NAACP.* New York: Atheneum, 1972.

Sheldon, Garett Ward. *The Political Philosophy of Thomas Jefferson.* Baltimore: Johns Hopkins University Press, 1991.

Stephano, Henrico, ed. *Thesaurus Graecae Linguae.* Vols. 1–2. Paris: Exudent Ambrosius Firmin Didot, 1831–1856.

Stuckey, Sterling. *Slave Culture: Nationalist Theory and the Foundations of Black America.* New York: Oxford University Press, 1987.

Thompson, Lloyd A. *Romans and Blacks.* Norman: University of Oklahoma Press, 1989.

Tuana, Nancy. *Woman and the History of Philosophy.* New York: Paragon Press, 1992.

Tucker, William H. *The Science and Politics of Racial Research.* Urbana: University of Illinois Press, 1994.

Wallace, Michele. *Black Macho and the Myth of the Superwoman.* New York: Warner Books, 1979.

Washington, Booker T. "An Address before the Afro-American Council." In *The Booker T. Washington Papers.* Vol. 7, *1903–4,* edited by Louis R. Harlan and Raymond Smock. Urbana: University of Illinois Press, 1977.

Washington, Booker T. *Up from Slavery.* New York: Oxford University Press, 1995.

West, Cornel. *Race Matters.* Boston: Beacon Press, 1993.

Williams, George Washington. *History of the Negro Race in America from 1619 to 1880.* Vol. 1. New York: Bergman, 1968.

Wilson, William Julius. *The Declining Significance of Race: Blacks and Changing American Institutions.* 2d ed. Chicago: University of Chicago Press, 1980.

Wright, W. D. *Black Intellectuals, Black Cognition, and a Black Aesthetic.* Westport, Conn.: Praeger, 1997.

Wright, W. D. "The Faces of Racism." *Western Journal of Black Studies* 11, no. 4 (1987): 168–176.

Wright, W. D. *Racism Matters.* Westport, Conn.: Praeger, 1998.

Wyatt, Gail Elizabeth. *Stolen Woman: Reclaiming Our Sexuality, Taking Back Our Lives.* New York: John Wiley & Sons, 1997.

Yee, Shirley J. *Black Women Abolitionists: A Study in Activism, 1828–1860.* Knoxville: University of Tennessee Press, 1992.

Yetman, Norman P., ed. *Life under the "Peculiar Institution": Selections from the Slave Narrative Collection.* New York: Holt, Rinehart, and Winston, 1970.

Index

ABOUT THE AUTHOR

W. D. Wright is Professor Emeritus of History at Southern Connecticut State University.